Financial Literacy for Beginners and Dummies

By Giovanni Rigters

Table of Contents

Introduction

Personal finance is crucial for anyone who wishes to achieve financial freedom. Managing money and planning our finances for different stages and situations is sensible if we don't want to find ourselves in a mess. Those who lack this management or planning skill often end up feeling lost. They struggle to pay off their debts and stay on top of their bills. Educating yourself in financial knowledge is a life skill necessary to have if you don't want to live your entire life living paycheck to paycheck. Even if you manage to make ends meet, an emergency, such as a medical problem or car crash, can dent your pocket. Your financial situation can improve drastically when you know how to budget your money and learn to invest it in the right places.

Unfortunately, financial literacy is not something that we are taught at school. Our perception of money is influenced by our upbringing, experiences, and daily observances. This is why many of us cultivate very toxic relationships with money. Because financial literacy isn't taught to us like history, math, or literature, we need to take it upon ourselves to enhance our monetary knowledge. Taking steps to improve your financial wellness is crucial. This is because our financial situation can deeply influence our physical, mental, and emotional health.

If you're reading this book, then this means that you've taken steps to get yourself on the right track! It is perfect for beginners who wish to get their finances together and improve the overall quality of their lives. You will have learned everything you need to know when you've read this book. We cover basic financial and economic concepts, like how to assess your current financial situation and how market prices are decided (and how this influences our buying decisions), to more complex subjects like choosing the right bank for your needs and where to invest your money.

You'll also become familiar with different types of insurance, understand how to draw up financial plans, find out what passive income is and how to achieve it, and come across some financial tools that you can use to aid you throughout your journey. Most importantly, reading this book will help you enrich your financial mindset.

This book serves as the ultimate financial guide for beginners who wish to transform their lives. Here, you will find all the instructions you need to make better money-related decisions. It is easy to read and understand. You don't have to worry about getting lost in a sea of financial jargon and complex calculations.

Once you read this book, you will realize that becoming financial literate is just the same as learning any other subject. You need to internalize all the information you need and then apply all this knowledge to become more skilled and competent. With practice, making better choices will eventually come as second nature to you. By investing in your financial literacy, you invest in your security and needs. You will learn how to budget, save, invest, and spend your money, stimulate cash flow, ward off outstanding debts, and grow your assets.

Chapter 1: What Is Finance?

If you're a hockey fan, you probably know Wayne Gretzky, the man who is widely acclaimed as the greatest player in NHL history. Several years ago, there were technical issues with the stadium lights during a game between the Edmonton Oilers and Boston Bruins. The game was paused as the technical team worked to find a solution. To use this wasted time, the game announcers started interviewing a few of the audience and the players. Unsurprisingly, Gretzky, the best player of all time, was interviewed too. When he was asked how he got his title even though he wasn't the strongest, toughest, or fastest in the league, he only had one thing to say: "I don't go where the puck is; I go where the puck is going to be!"

You're probably wondering if this story has anything to do with finance. Well, sometimes, the best advice comes from where it's least expected. Finance is all about the future. It is how you manage your expenses regardless of past financial habits, decisions, and market trends. Like Gretzky, you need to anticipate where the "puck" will be when you're making future financial considerations.

We can say with much confidence that the most successful analysts, business people, and investors are those who anticipate where the puck is going to be so they can get there first. They predict the market's direction so they can plan their finances accordingly. Instead of following everyone else (probably those who make their decisions based on previous experiences and markers), they lead the market.

What Is Finance?

Finance is the study or science of managing large sums of money. It is a huge umbrella used to reference any activities that have to do with investing, leveraging, capital, credit, markets, banking, and credit. Finance is also used to describe and direct the process of acquiring the funds. This is where the phrase "finance a business, car, house, etc." comes from.

Most basic financial concepts, which we will be discussing in more depth throughout this chapter, are derived from macroeconomic and microeconomic theories. The "value of money" is one of the most remarkable theories. This one suggests that the value of the dollar today is higher than it will be in the future.

The study of finance can be divided into three categories: personal, corporate, and government, or public finance. The financial services sector drives a country's economy. This is the sector where businesses and customers interact to acquire financial goods. It acts as an intermediate where savers (consumers) offer funds to financial services (banks, stock brokerages, insurance companies, and other institutions and instruments) so they can lend them to borrowers (businesses, households, or the government).

Subcategories of Finance

Households (individuals and families), businesses, and governments can't operate if they don't have enough funding.

Corporate Finance

Corporate finance accounts for the financial activities that any business, corporation, or private institute conducts. These financial activities are associated with the operation and running of a business. The company typically has a team or an entire department responsible for overseeing and managing those financial activities.

For instance, a situation relating to corporate finance would be a business determining if it should raise the needed bonds by offering stocks to the public or issuing bonds. Corporations may seek out the guidance of investment banks to help them make these financial decisions and aid them in the marketing activities related to the securities.

Another example would be the capital that the startups need to operate their business. In that case, they can get the needed capital via venture capitalists or angel investors. In exchange, startups offer them a decided percentage of ownership. If this business wishes to grow and become a public corporation, it will issue shares on the stock exchange market. This can be done through an IPO, or initial public offering, allowing them to raise capital.

While it can be very challenging, especially if the cost of running the startup is high, it may try to budget and save its capital. It will identify areas of the business that need financing, prioritize them, and decide which ones can be put off for later. This will allow those in charge to work towards priorities for the company's growth first, then tackle the next steps.

Public Finance

Public or government finance refers to a government's budgeting, spending, debt insurance, and tax policies. These policies influence the government's ability and the methods they use so it can pay for all the public services provided for its citizens. Public finance falls under the macroeconomic concept of fiscal policy, which refers to the impact tax policies and government spending have on economic activities like employment, the aggregate or overall demand for goods and services, inflation, economic growth, and inflation.

A government's financial decisions and activities help it prevent a market failure. The state does so by managing the allocation of resources, overseeing the distribution of income, and maintaining general economic stability. Most of a government's funding comes from its tax policies. The state may often resort to borrowing from the public via banks or insurance companies. Governments can also seek funding from other countries.

Besides managing the flow of money in regular daily operations, the state also oversees other fiscal and social activities and services. Since citizens, particularly those who are obliged to pay taxes, participate in fulfilling a government's funding needs, the state is expected to offer adequate social programs in return. It is also expected to maintain economic stability to reinforce trust and eliminate uncertainty among its people. Taxpayers need a guarantee that their money is safe and that they can save for the future.

Personal Finance

You're probably most concerned with personal finance if you're reading this book. When households participate in financial planning activities, they consider their current financial standing. This allows them to develop strategies that help them meet their future needs within their financial limitations. Personal finance refers to an individual's or a household's current financial activities and standing. These plans are highly dependent on a person's income, the standard of living, wants, needs, and goals.

For instance, people need to take into account their retirement plans. To properly prepare for retirement, they need to make sure that they're saving up and investing enough money during their working years to finance their long-term plans. Personal finance comprises a wide array of activities, including investing in financial goods, such as insurance, credit cards, and mortgages. Banking also falls under the category of personal finance because households use Venmo, PayPal, and other mobile or e-payment services, savings accounts, and checking accounts.

What Are Financial Services?

As mentioned above, financial services are the processes or intermediaries via which households and companies obtain financial goods. To simplify things, let's take a look at the financial service that a payment system provides. This service facilitates transactions between the person who pays and the entity that receives the funds. The function of this service is to accept and receive transfers between those parties and comprises accounts settled through debit cards, checks, credit cards, and electronic funds transfers.

The financial services industry makes up one of the vital aspects of the economy. Without financial services, the economy wouldn't be able to operate. This sector drives liquidity and the free flow of capital in a nation's market. Finance companies, lenders, insurance companies, real estate brokers, investment houses, accounting services, and banks are just a few financial institutes that make up this sector.

This is an essential sector because it aids in the maintenance of a nation's economy. When both the economy and this sector are strong, the trust, assurance, and certainty of consumers or households rise and their purchasing power. Similarly, when this industry declines, the economy declines, dragging the nation into a state of economic recession.

It must be noted that financial goods and financial services are not the same. Financial services are not owned and can't be separated from their provider. For instance, receiving advice on your investments from a professional, having someone manage your investments, or receiving any other services provided by a financial advisor are all examples of financial services. On the other hand, financial products are things that you can own, such as insurance policies, stocks and bonds, and mortgages.

What Are Financial Activities?

Financial activities are any process, transactions, and strategies that companies, households, and governments take so they can take steps toward achieving their economic goals. These activities typically revolve around the flow of money, whether they are inflow transactions (receiving money) or outflows (spending). Purchasing and selling assets or products, offering and receiving loans, keeping accounts, and issuing stocks are all examples of financial activities. Examples of a company's financial activities include repaying debts and offering shares. Households and governments participate in financial transactions (activities) when taxes are levied, or loans are taken out.

Economic Concepts You Need to Know

The study of finance is driven by and derived from economics. While finance asses several components of the financial systems, such as credit, investment, cash, and banking, economics is the study of the consumption, distribution, and production of goods and services in a market. Its main concern is the behavior and the financial interaction between the players in any economy: households, governments, and businesses.

There are two subcategories of economics: macroeconomics and microeconomics. Macroeconomics focuses on the performance of an economy as a whole, while microeconomics is concerned with single factors of the economy and the impact of their individual decisions. Financial economics refers to analyzing markets and assessing how their resources are used and distributions. Economic theories evaluate how risks, opportunity costs, time, and certain information can affect an entity's financial decision.

We know what you're probably thinking: "I am here to learn how to budget for my household's needs, save for my retirement plan, or make better investment decisions. How will understanding economic theories help me?" Well, as dramatic as this may sound, the essence of economics influences every aspect of our lives. The proof here is that fundamentally, economics aims to explain the reasons behind our financial choices.

Understanding the reasons behind your financial decisions is the key to making better spending choices. The following concepts can help you understand why you make the financial choices you do:

Scarcity

Scarcity is a concept that everyone understands because we've all experienced its impact in one way or another. As you can guess from the term, scarcity references one of the most common and basic economic problems to exist. That is having fewer or limited resources in comparison to the world's unlimited wants. No matter how many resources there are, there will never be enough to meet the world's infinite desires. This is why we are all obliged to allocate our resources as efficiently as possible. Making smart financial and budgeting decisions would allow us to ensure that our highest priorities are always met.

For instance, let's say there is only so much land that we can plant every year. While some people want apples, others want cucumbers. Only a limited amount of either good can be produced because of the scarcity of agricultural land. So, how do those in charge determine how much land to allocate to plant apples and cucumbers? The only way to decide is by examining the concept of supply and demand, the drivers of a market system.

Supply and Demand

Supply and demand are what drive a market system. Let's take the example above. When many people are willing to buy apples at a given price, the demand for apples is relatively high. This is why apple sellers are prompted to charge more for them. Charging a higher price allows them to make more profit and meet the rising demand. Farmers who plant the apples will also charge the sellers more for the fruit and will be compelled to allocate more land to planting apples than cucumbers.

In most cases, other people will want to start selling apples too (or the goods in the high demand), so they can also profit. As a result, there will be plenty of apples in the market after a couple of production cycles. People then will expect to pay a lower price for the apples because they're so abundant now. Additionally, supply is a lot higher than demand at that point (production surplus), so fewer apples will be produced. The supply of apples decreases, and so does the price.

Even though the concept of supply and demand is very simplified in this example, you can still understand how supply and demand work together to determine the price of goods. You can also see why many popular products are almost half the price after a year or so.

Costs and Benefits

Economics is based on a very important theory: the concept of rational choice and expectations. This theory plays a huge role in how we make our financial decisions, as it's related to how we measure a product's (or service's) cost against its benefits. In economics, rational behavior refers to an individual's effort to maximize the ratio of costs to benefits when they make any financial decision.

For example, landowners will hire more workers to plant or harvest apples if there's high demand. However, this would work only in the case if the selling price of apples, along with the number of apples being sold, were worth the additional costs incurred by the landowner. Higher wages, more advanced agricultural technology, and perhaps land expansions are examples of these costs. Similarly, customers will search for the highest quality of apples they can afford to buy (fresh, pesticide-free, firm, lack discolorations, etc.) but not necessarily pay for organic apples sold at specialty grocers.

This concept is not limited to financial decisions, which shows how far the study of economics is involved in our lives. For instance, you perform a cost-benefit analysis whenever you prioritize a certain task over another. Because it's important that we act rationally and maximize the ratio of costs to benefits, it's important to realize whenever we aren't ratios. Daily advertisements and marketing tactics can trick us into overestimating the benefits of purchasing a certain good or service.

Incentives

As humans, we are all inclined to perform better when offered a reward or an incentive. On an economic level, the interaction of supply and demand in the market can act as an incentive for producers to offer the goods that households want and for households to preserve scarce resources. As you know by now, prices rise when demand increasesso suppliers have the incentive to supply more of that commodity because they can now make more profits. However, this increase in supply and demand prompts scarcity of raw material, and so, the cost to produce that good rises, causing suppliers to supply less. The price of the goods rises even more, and so consumers will now have an incentive to cut back on their consumption. Consumers will never pay more for a product than its esteemed value of it.

In the example of an apple seller, the landowner wants to increase the production of apples. One way to do that would be offering an incentive, or a raise in wages, to the farmers who harvest the most apples in a given timeframe. In a couple of weeks, the number of apples produced rises. The problem here is that the landowner offered the incentive for the number of apples produced rather than their quality. The store owner that the landowner supplies called to complain about the quality of the apples he received. Because the higher wages were offered for the number of apples harvested, farmers found it more efficient to pick the apples slightly earlier than they were supposed to. This is why people should be careful and precise when offering incentives. They should align with the individual's or business' goals.

What Is Financial Literacy and Why Is It Important?

Financial literacy refers to an individual's knowledge regarding managing their credit, finances, and debt. All responsible and rational decisions are based on your level of financial literacy. These decisions include but aren't limited to setting up a budget, knowing how to use different financial tools and when to refer to financial institutes and professionals, and paying off debt. In short, financial literacy has a huge influence on an individual's ability to make ends meet, cover their priorities and basic needs, finance their kid's education, purchase a home, and plan out their retirement.

Many people, even those who live in advanced economies, struggle with financial illiteracy. There are people across the world who don't grasp basic financial concepts, which is why they have trouble maintaining a certain standard of living. Generally speaking, the higher the lack of financial literacy in an economy, the poorer the overall nation is. However, it's still worth noting that even though income levels and the quality of education influence a person's level of financial literacy, it was found that many high-income and educated households maintain the same level of financial ignorance as the less fortunate. Thinking about financial issues and matters can be incredibly stress-inducing and anxiety-triggering, which can be very troublesome for many people.

As you can probably already tell, financial literacy is vital because it allows people to make informed decisions when it comes to handling their finances. Additionally, the number of financial burdens and responsibilities that fall on an individual increases over time. At the most basic level, past employers managed their employee's retirement accounts. Nowadays, however, self-directed retirement accounts shift this responsibility over to employees. The number of financial options and products available has also increased greatly. Credit can also be accessed more easily. This means that the number of choices that an individual has to make is greater.

In this chapter, we covered what finance as a study is and the main economic factors that influence our financial decisions. You better understand how the interplay of supply and demand impacts price levels, a producer's willingness to supply, and a consumer's willingness to produce. You also understand the importance of financial literacy, which is something that this book is guaranteed to help you grow.

Chapter 2: Your Financial Mindset

Your financial health is just as relevant as your physical, mental, and emotional health. This is because your financial situation can greatly impact your overall well-being. Checking up on your finances every now and then can help you determine the areas in your life you need to adjust, budget for, or manage more efficiently.

In this chapter, we will help you assess where you stand financially. Knowing where you stand in terms of your will give you a starting point from which you grow to achieve your financial goals. Here, you will understand whether your relationship with money is holding you back and how you can improve how you view and use money. Finally, you'll learn how to set monetary goals and track your spending in this chapter.

Where Do You Stand, Financially?

When was the last time you took a step back and evaluated your financial situation? Well, if you're reading this book, the chances are that you aren't happy with your financial position in life. However, did you actually take the time to identify which habits you need to get rid of or what smart financial behaviors you need to start adopting? Financial issues can wreak havoc on mental, emotional, and physical health. This is why we always need to be aware of our financial standing. Checking up on your financial activities, from income to spending and everything in between, can help you make the necessary changes. This is why we are here to tell you the five most important steps you need to take when evaluating your financial well-being.

Consider Your Net Worth

When evaluating your financial health, you need to determine your net worth. This is a quick and easy way to evaluate your current financial position. All you need to do is to find the sum of the value of all your assets and then subtract your liabilities. Grab a piece of paper and think about everything you own, whether your home, car, cash, or investments. Then, subtract all you consider a liability (debts you need to pay). This can be your credit card debt, pending mortgage payments, student loans, etc. It's important to note that your income shouldn't be included when you're calculating your net worth. This exercise is no more than a mere indicator of what you own and what you owe.

The best thing about calculating your net worth is that it allows you to compare yourself, not to others, but to yourself. This way, you can easily determine if your financial situation is improving or deteriorating. Let's say that your home is your only asset, to make things simple. Assume your home is worth $250,000 and you have $200,000 worth of liabilities. In that case, your net worth would be $50,000. Your net worth grows as you cover more and more of your mortgage. This is assuming that the value of your home doesn't decrease. Don't get discouraged if your net worth is

25

currently a negative number. The only point behind calculating it is so you can keep track of it regularly. Think of it as a personal financial unit of measurement. It will help you understand how well you're using your money.

Remember that everyone's opportunities and circumstances are unique, which is why you should never compare your net worth to that of others. As a good rule of thumb, set a goal to increase your net worth by 5-10% each year. Then, calculate how much of your debt you need to cover to reach that goal.

Find Out Your Debt-to-Income Ratio

Now that you've calculated your net worth, you can actually account for your income. To calculate your debt-to-income ratio, you need to divide your monthly gross income by the amount of money you pay in debt repayments. For instance, if your monthly gross income pre-tax deductions (and other possible deductions) is $8,000 and you have a monthly $2000 mortgage payment, $200 to pay for your car, another $200 for your student loans, and a $100 in credit card payments. In that case, your total debt payments would be $2500, and your debt-to-ratio income would be 31.25%. Maintaining a ratio of 30% is highly recommended by lenders, and people, in general. However, to stay on the safe side, aim for 20% or lower.

Calculating this ratio allows you to work out if you are managing your debt properly. You should start worrying if your ratio is at 40-50%. This ratio is a key factor in terms of your credit score. The higher the ratio, the fewer the mortgage lenders will be who will agree to work with you.

Can You Afford Your Home?

Forty percent of the average American's budget is spent on housing alone, as per 2017 data. For instance, if someone earns an annual salary of $70000, they end up paying $28000 on housing. Alarming, right? Remember the housing crisis that happened in 2008? To avoid another crisis, the only solution is for people to start living in houses they can afford.

When determining how much you pay for housing, you need to remember there is more to account for than just your mortgage payment. For instance, you will have to pay for transportation to and from work, despite the cheaper rent payment, if you live somewhere outside the city. If you live in the heart of the city, you may not have to pay as much for commuting, but you'll probably pay a premium rental. If your calculations reveal that you're paying too much for housing, consider moving to a more affordable place or finding a roommate to share your costs with.

Track Your Spending

Many people overlook the importance of budgeting their money. At most, they ensure they don't draw more money than they can afford to and save as much money as they can each month. However, if you want to reach your financial goals, you need to know where each penny is coming from and where you will be spending it. Even though this may sound unreasonable and time-consuming, it's the only way you'll ever move forward. You can do that by setting up a budget and making sure that you stick to it. Know what you want to spend on each category (food, clothes, rent, etc.) to come up with a budget that suits your income. You can be flexible in the sense that you can move your money around from one category to the other. The ultimate goal is not to spend more than the amount of money you've budgeted for the month while managing to cover your needs. After determining where your money is going, you can set up a suitable budget. You need to ensure that you allocate an amount toward your savings.

Set Goals

You need to set financial goals for yourself, which we will discuss in more depth throughout the chapter. This is the most critical thing you can do when checking up on your financial wellness. Your goals will serve as a mark that you can measure your performance against.

Improving Your Relationship with Money

Money is not something that people normally talk about. We are never taught the basics of money management and financial literacy in school. Unless people decide to learn about money themselves, just like you're doing now, experience and observations are your only sources of learning. Our understanding of money is shaped by our friends, family, and community from a very young age. Overhearing a conversation about someone's finances or receiving information via sources of information can also influence the way we view money. All of these external sources combine in our subconscious to form what is known as our "money identity."

People who often hear their parents say that they can't afford certain stuff grow up believing that money is a scarce resource. This is why they often feel guilty when they spend money and don't like spending it. Those who grow up in communities where having money was deemed as unimportant or owning a vehicle was indicative of greed or laziness tend to disregard the financial side of life altogether. These are all examples of limiting beliefs. Once you grow up and get away from these influential factors, one would think that you can develop your own money identity. However, unfortunately, the opposite usually happens, and these beliefs grow more and more powerful.

Having a bad relationship with money can impact plenty of areas of your life. Depending on where the issue lies, you may struggle with saving money, paying off debts, overspending, or even underspending. Limiting money beliefs can trick you into believing that you will never be able to handle your money rationally. So, if no one ever speaks about money, how do you fix your relationship with it?

Understand That Money Is a Tool

The key to building a good relationship with money is to view it as no more than a tool. Tools, like hammers, can be helpful or destructive, depending on how you use them. If you don't know how to use a hammer, you'll probably break everything you land it on. If you know how to use it, you can build amazing things. Knowing how to use money can help you build the life you desire. Money mismanagement, on the other hand, can be detrimental.

Don't Complicate It

Money is not hard to understand. Understanding how it works and how you can use it for your greater good is not beyond you. Any steps toward improving your financial literacy will help you move toward your goals.

Challenge Your Money Identity

It's easy to let our upbringing and previous experiences shape our perception of money. Instead of letting your parents' beliefs about money influence yours, take the time to observe and learn from how they managed their money. Why was money scarce in your household? Were they having trouble saving their money? Did they have clear financial goals? Did they believe that financial wellness only came with certain types of jobs? Did they not budget their income efficiently?

Use Positive Money Affirmations

Our subconscious leads us to believe the phrases that we repeat over and over again. For instance, the more you talk negatively about your finances and your lack of ability to manage them, the more you'll believe that you can never change your financial situation. Therefore, you will probably never consider taking steps to improve your finances. Similarly, when you use positive statements, such as "I can achieve my money goals" or "I am capable of overcoming financial challenges," your relationship with money will improve significantly.

Believe That You Can Change Your Financial Situation

Your financial situation may not be ideal at the moment. This can be discouraging. However, it helps to remember that this can change if you get a raise, find a better job, or start saving diligently. You will never feel good about your relationship with money if you don't start believing that all life situations are temporary. There will come periods in life when you are strapped for cash and others when you don't have to worry about rewarding yourself with a trip or something expensive that you've been eyeing. The difference is that when you know how to use your money, you will learn how to deal with financial pitfalls or even avoid them altogether.

Stop Comparing

Nothing ruins our relationship with ourselves and other things in life like comparisons. Our sense of self-worth and accomplishment is hindered when we compare our progress to that of others. We struggle with self-love and confidence when we compare our appearance to that of others. We feel less financially secure when we compare our standard of living with that of others. That trip to Bali that your friend is posting about or the luxurious home that your neighbor lives in doesn't suggest that they're excelling in life and you're not. Everyone's journey and circumstances are different.

Setting Financial Goals and Achieving Them

Many people try their best to improve their financial situation but see no progress whatsoever. They slave away at work, but it never seems to pay off. This is because they don't know what they want to achieve. You already know that you need to have financial goals if you want to improve your money situation.

Financial goals are any plans that you have regarding your money. You can set goals for a year, five, or ten years from now, as long as your plan is rational and feasible. Here's how you can set financial goals and stick to them.

Write Down Your Goals

Did you know that you are more likely to achieve your goals when you write them down? Many people feel committed when they write things down because they're no longer random thoughts or floating commitments. You can hold yourself accountable by writing down your goals and putting them somewhere visible.

Be Specific

When you set a goal for yourself, you need to be specific. Don't just write down, "I want to improve my financial situation." Instead, you need to narrow it down. Figure out which aspects of your financial situation you'd like to change, prioritize them. Let's say your goals are to buy a home and pay off your debts. It would make more sense to tackle the latter first.

They Have to Be Measurable and Time-Bound

If you have a large sum in outstanding debt, you'll need to break this amount into smaller numbers. Then, decide on the deadlines or timeframes you need to have those debts paid off. For instance, you can write down "I will pay off $10000 of debt by January 2023" instead of "I will pay off most of my debt soon." Setting a specific amount of money can help you measure whether you've achieved your goal. Your goals and deadlines should be challenging but not impossible to achieve.

They Should Be Your Own Goals

We all tend to get swayed by what everyone else is doing in life. It's easy to overhear your friend say that they're saving up to buy a car, and you immediately think: "oh... I should buy a car too." If you've never thought about purchasing one until that moment, then you probably don't need it now. Your goals should be about you and your needs.

Setting financial goals for yourself can help improve your relationship with money. All the points we've discussed in this chapter are related to each other. Doing these things will prompt you to analyze all your financial decisions and realize how all your choices impact your financial well-being. The way you use and view your money impacts every aspect of your being. It affects your mental, physical, and emotional health. How secure we are with our finances also dictates our social relationships and interactions. This is why financial literacy is one of the most important skills anyone can obtain.

Chapter 3: Creating a Financial Plan

A financial plan will help secure your future. The days of guaranteeing the future could be long gone, and the uncertain times we live in could be the new normal; however, we need to be prepared as best as we can. We all have financial goals and objectives, and a successful financial plan can help us achieve these goals. When you have a strategy, you have a path to follow to manage your finances which will, in turn, help you secure your future. It doesn't matter how old you are or what stage of life you are at; we all need to create a financial plan right now; the sooner, the better.

What Is a Financial Plan?

A financial plan is a documented analysis that gives you a clear picture of your current finances, assets, investments, and liabilities. It also allows you to prioritize your objectives and provides you with strategies to achieve your financial goals. The plan should include all the details related to your finances like your cash flow, debts, savings, insurance, and so on.

It is impossible to meet someone nowadays who isn't stressed about money unless they are a Hollywood star or football player. We are all struggling to figure out what we should do to be financially secure and save for the future. A clear financial plan will put you on the right track by allowing you to take advantage of your assets and adjust your expenses to meet your objectives.

You won't be able to meet your financial goals if you don't have an insight into your finances that can inform you whether or not you are on the right track with your savings or if you need to change your spending habits. A financial plan can be long-term, especially if you plan for your retirement, or short-term for a few months if your goal is in the near future. Financial plans aren't fixed; you can always make any changes to them if you encounter any unexpected expenses like a hospital stay or having a child.

Some people think that creating a financial plan isn't for them because of the misconception that you have to be wealthy to plan your finances. However, everyone can benefit from a financial plan, no matter their financial situation. In fact, it can help you grow your income and increase your wealth in the long run.

Why You Need a Financial Plan

Security

One of the main reasons people create financial plans is to secure their future, especially if they have a family. Planning your finances allows you to manage your money better, thus increasing your savings. You will be able to financially cover any unexpected expenses that life throws at you, like losing your job or unplanned pregnancy. Having money set aside for emergencies will provide you and your family with financial security.

Growing Your Income

A financial plan will help you keep track of your income and expenses to grow your money and achieve your financial goals. As your income grows, so will your cash flow. Monitoring your daily spending habits will make you aware of your daily expenses to cut down any necessary expenses and focus on your priorities. You become more in control of your finances and thus develop better and smarter spending habits.

Invest Your Money

Once you become aware of your income and expenses and start saving money, you can find the right investment that will help you to expand your wealth and achieve your financial goals.

Preparing for Inflation

The world has become uncertain, and many current events have led to rampant inflation. It has become the fact that we just can't escape. The value of money has been declining and will continue to do so. A financial plan will help you deal with inflation as you prepare for your future and, hopefully, a retirement without any no financial worries.

Achieving Your Goals

We all have long-term goals like buying a house or a car. Saving money to achieve these goals isn't easy unless you have a clear plan and a time period that you set for yourself.

Manage Your Debt

Many of us get into debt as a result of taking loans from banks to buy a home or make any big purchases, and we also can't forget about credit card debt. Without a careful financial plan, debt can turn into a financial crisis. As mentioned, a financial plan will allow you to track your expenses and income, save money, and pay your debt.

Retirement

You will need to have a stable income next to your pension to afford to have a comfortable lifestyle after retirement. A financial plan will help you save enough money for your future life after you retire. Financial planning will provide you with a secure and brighter future.

How to Create a Successful Personal Financial Plan

Young people can fall into the trap of thinking that it's too early to start planning for their future, and a lot of older people think it is too late, so there is no point. However, in all seriousness, it is never too late or too early to start planning your finances for a better tomorrow. So now that you know what a financial plan is and why it is necessary to have one, we will discuss how to create a successful personal financial plan.

Assess Your Current Situation

You shouldn't start planning without first assessing your current financial situation. We pay our monthly requirements as if by habit, without paying attention to the amount of money we are spending. So, take a moment to check your bank statements to see how much you pay for rent, gas, electricity, bank charges, Netflix etc., for the last year. Naturally, you will notice some irregular spending. This will point out the unnecessary expenses you will need to cut down.

You should also determine your net worth by subtracting your liabilities (mortgage, loans, or debts) from your assets (car, home, and the money in your bank account). Your net worth will normally change, for instance, when you pay off your debt or buy a new home, so you should keep track of it. If your assets are larger than your liabilities, then you have a good net worth.

Set Financial Goals

Once you become aware of your net worth and unnecessary expenses, you can start with the first step of your financial planning, which is setting your financial goals. This is a vital step as it will point you in the right direction. Setting S.M.A.R.T (Specific Measurable Attainable Relevant Time-bound) goals is best. Your purpose shouldn't simply be "saving money"; it has to be more specific and detailed than that. How much money do you want to save? Why do you need this money? When should this money be ready? Is your goal long-term or short-term? This is how you set S.M.A.R.T goals.

You will also need to figure out your goals by treating yourself like you are in a job interview and asking yourself this tough question "where do you see yourself in 5, 10, or 20 years?" The answer to this question will help you put into perspective your priorities. For instance, do you see yourself as a homeowner? Living abroad? Starting a family? Once you decide where you want to be, you can start planning your finances accordingly.

We all have different goals, and saving for all of them at once may not be realistic. So, consider the most important ones you will need at this stage of your life. For instance, if you are starting a family and need a bigger home, it makes sense to prioritize saving for a home over saving for retirement. If you can save for two goals at once, this will be ideal, like saving for your children's college and retirement plan. Simply put, set your priorities straight. Paying your debt takes precedence over saving for retirement but saving for retirement is more important than saving for traveling.

So, make a list of all the things you hope to achieve, whether buying a new car or even buying an expensive sweater. Seeing your goals put down on paper will keep you motivated so that you can turn them into a reality.

Consider Your Debt

How will you be able to save money if you are paying off your debt? For this reason, we recommend you pay off your debt first. Include your debt in your financial plan and figure out a way to get rid of this burden ASAP. Remember, fees and interest rates with debt usually add to your expenses, so the sooner you pay them off, the better. When you are debt-free, you will have the financial freedom to save money to achieve your goals.

Create a Budget

Creating a budget is another vital step that will help you achieve your financial objectives. That said, you can't just create a budget; you must also stick to it. U.S. Senator Elizabeth Warren has come up with a great way to set a budget by dividing your income (after taxes) into three categories: 20% for savings, 30% for your wants, and 50% for the essentials. We will discuss in detail how to create a budget in the next chapter.

Create an Emergency Fund

Having a financial plan means that you will always be prepared for emergencies that would require unexpected expenses, which can impact your financial objectives. Many of us live paycheck to paycheck, so we aren't prepared in case of accidents or illness. Having a financial safety net will come in handy in the case of emergencies like losing your job. The amount of money you should put aside for emergencies will depend on your expenses. So, make sure to save an amount that will last you for six months. Establishing an emergency fund is necessary if your job or career isn't stable or you have a poor credit score.

As we have mentioned, we live in uncertain times. Many people have lost their jobs as a result of COVID-19, and now we are suffering the impact of war, so we don't know what the future holds. This is why you should set money aside to provide you with peace of mind during these unpredictable times. So, you must include an emergency fund in your financial plan.

Consider Investment

Many people consider saving their money, but only a few consider investing this money. The investment will help you increase your wealth and give you security for when you retire. We will discuss how to invest your money later on in the book.

Estate Planning

No one of us wants to think of death, but we need to make sure that our loved ones are taken care of when we aren't here. You don't have to be rich or an elderly citizen to start estate planning. Include it in your financial plan now to have peace of mind and guarantee the protection of your loved ones. Your estate plan should include power of attorney, last will and testament, trust information, and healthcare directives.

The first step in estate planning is to write down your will and assets and decide who will be trusted with this information. This is a big step with so much on the line, so we suggest you hire a lawyer to help you out.

Insurance

You may not see it now, but insurance is actually an investment. It will protect your health and assets and even ensure your family is provided for when you aren't around anymore. There are various types of insurance, but we suggest you focus on the essential ones: health insurance, life insurance, disability insurance, homeowner's insurance, and auto insurance. Insurance is just like an emergency fund that will prevent you from dipping into your savings in case of an emergency.

Consider Your Taxes

No one enjoys doing their taxes, and they can be very confusing. Figuring out how taxes work will help you with achieving your long-term goals. There are two essential things that you should consider when you are planning your taxes: itemizing your deductions and reducing your taxable income.

Itemizing your deductions will allow you to reduce your taxable income as someone who is self-employed, working part-time, or full-time. You will be able to lower your taxable income by deducting incurred costs from doing business. Taking advantage of tax-saving investing options like 401 K and 403 B will also help you lower your taxable income to save money.

Plan for Your Retirement

As we've said, it's never too early to start planning and preparing for your retirement. In fact, the earlier you start saving, the better your older self will be grateful that you have decided to take this crucial step now. The younger you start, the longer you will have to save money and thus secure your future. However, if you start at an older age, you should put more money in your retirement fund. We suggest you save about 10 to 15 percent of your income (after tax) every year for your retirement.

Keep Track of Your Plan

Financial plans aren't cast in stone, and your goals can change along the way, and so will your plan. For this reason, you should review your plan regularly and make the necessary adjustments. For instance, as you grow older and advance in your career, your income will increase, so you can increase the amount you set aside each month for your savings as well. Additionally, keeping track of your financial plan will prevent you from skipping payments every once in a while to ensure you stick to your goals. You should also reevaluate your plan after big financial ventures like having kids or buying a new car. Reviewing your plan will allow you to keep track of your progress which will help keep you motivated. Additionally, you will be able to notice if there are any issues that you need to work on, like eating out less so you can reduce your expenses. You should also seek the help of a financial advisor to help guide you through the process and provide advice when necessary.

An Example of a Financial Plan

Your personal financial plan must include this information:

- All your personal information (age, children, tax filing status, income, etc.)

- Your financial goals which include your assets and debt as well

- A plan for your debt elimination

- An investment plan to increase your wealth

- Insurance

- An estate plan

- Income tax strategies

Creating a financial plan is a big step toward securing your future. There are many benefits to creating a financial plan to help you achieve your long-term and short-term goals. However, you should take your plan very seriously and stick to it. Make it a habit to always set a specific amount of money aside for the future. Set your priorities straight and focus on your main goals. Financial planning is all about having a secure future for you and your loved ones. You will be able to take care of any emergencies or unexpected expenses that come your way. Most of all, you should always review your plan. You won't be able to determine if your financial plan is working or not if you don't regularly check it. This will give you the chance to make the necessary adjustments in case you aren't making any progress.

Your future starts now. Take the step today and start planning your finances for a better and brighter tomorrow. Remember, it is never too late or too early to start planning for your future.

Chapter 4: Budgeting and Saving

We've gone over how budgeting is an essential part of your finances in the previous chapters. It is a map that helps you see where your money is going and if you are overspending and need to make better decisions with your money. When you make a budget, you are essentially making a plan for how you will spend your money. This will help you pay off your debt, put some money aside for emergencies, and cover your expenses. A budget allows you to prioritize and set a spending limit so you can protect your finances and save for the future.

You may find sitting down and planning a budget tedious because you want to have fun and enjoy your hard-earned money like everyone else. However, this small inconvenience beats drowning in debt, and once done, you know where you are and how much you have to buy all the things you want and achieve your goals with the money you save.

The Importance of Budgeting

Controls Your Spending

Thanks to credit cards, we all spend money we don't have and on things we don't need in many cases. We end up in debt and have to figure out ways to pay it off. How do we expect to save money when we are living beyond our means? Credit cards don't allow us to keep track of our spending, resulting in overspending and debt. In fact, one of the biggest problems we have is that we let our money control us instead of the other way around.

Planning a budget and sticking to it will save you from this unnecessary pain. You will be able to control your spending and save money once you plan your monthly expenses in advance and don't go over your planned budget.

Improves Your Spending Habits

We don't usually pay attention to the amount of money we spend each month until we run out of it before the month ends or find ourselves in debt. Ask yourself, do you really need to eat out every day? Do you have to subscribe to every streaming service? If you take a look at your spending habits, you will realize there are many things that you are wasting your money on. A budget will show you the unnecessary expenses you make to improve your spending habits and develop real financial goals.

Keeps You Focused on Financial Goals

It isn't realistic to buy just anything you see and like at a store or eat at fancy restaurants every day. How will you be able to save to buy a house or to pay for college? Your goals are more important than satisfying your every whim, especially your long-term goals that will guarantee you live a comfortable and financially secure life. Planning a budget will help you stay motivated, disciplined, and focused on your long-term goals to create a secure future for yourself and your family.

Provides You with Security

As we have mentioned, life is filled with unexpected surprises, and you may find yourself having to pay for expenses that you haven't planned for. If you aren't careful with your money, you may end up in a financial crisis as a result. A budget will help you build an emergency fund to provide you and your family with security in case of any unfortunate event and give you peace of mind knowing you can financially support your family in any given situation.

How to Organize and Develop a Written Budget

You need to create a monthly budget to plan your expenses and savings for each month, track your progress, and, more importantly, get into the habit of being aware of your spending patterns. We understand that many people don't like to create a budget because they feel it is limiting, especially if you are young and want to spend your money. You are probably thinking, "leave budgeting for older people." However, a budget helps you plan a secure future, and you are never too young to start planning for tomorrow.

Before creating your budget, you should write down all the necessary information and be ruthlessly honest with yourself. We know it can be hard to face your spending habits. The truth may hurt, especially if you are an "over-spender" and weren't aware of it, but this is the only way you can create an effective budget and fix these habits.

Prepare the Necessary Paperwork

The first step is to prepare all the necessary paperwork to help you plan your budget. You will need bank statements, utility bills for the last couple of months, credit card bills, mortgage statements, 1099s, investment accounts, W-2s and pay stubs, and recent receipts.

Calculate Your Income

Calculating your income after tax is the most crucial step that you should take when preparing your budget. How much money do you make each month? This doesn't just include your salary but other sources like social security, child support, government benefits, or investments. If you are a business owner, you should include the money that goes into your pocket (the salary you give yourself), not how much money the business makes. If you are a freelancer or your income varies each month, include an average of what you earn.

Write Down Your Fixed Expenses

Write down all your mandatory expenses like rent, heat, electricity bill, internet, insurance, water, medication, child support, child care, alimony, car payment, student loan, and transportation. Many of these expenses are fixed, so you won't have to guess. Looking at your bank statement and receipts for the last couple of months will provide you with all the information you need. You should also include your debt if you have any.

Write Down Variable Expenses

Variable expenses are the expenses that change every month, like gas, groceries, and phone bills. Write down the average amount for each of these expenses, and check your bank or credit card statements for the last three to six months to make an estimate. You should also write down any unexpected expenses that you think might affect your budget.

Non-Essential Expenses

After adding all your essential expenses, you should now add the non-essential ones. They are usually the ones that aren't as necessary, and you may be able to give up or spend less money on them. These expenses include unnecessary clothing, gifts, eating out, house cleaning, streaming services subscription, travel, cable TV, home decor, personal grooming, and gym membership.

Your Monthly Expenses vs. Your Monthly Income

You will need to do some math to figure out which is higher: your monthly income or your monthly expenses. The ideal is if your income is higher because this means that you have enough money to cover all your expenses and put some on the side or to pay off your debt. In this case, you can apply the 50-30-20 method discussed in the previous chapter. However, if you have discovered that you spend more money than you make, you know you should make some serious changes to your spending habits.

Cut Down Unnecessary Expenses

How can you reduce your expenses and save some money? Focus on unnecessary expenses like eating out, having your hair done every week, or shopping for expensive clothes. Give up these things or make smarter buying decisions. For instance, if you need clothes, wait for sales or offers so you can buy more for less.

You must reach a point where your income covers all of your essential expenses with some to spare. However, if you are in debt, you may need to make more drastic changes. In this case, you will have to cut down some of your fixed expenses that aren't essential, like canceling your cable TV or streaming services subscription. You should also find a way to increase your income by working extra hours or getting a freelance job.

Use Your Budget

Now that you have created a budget, you should start using it. Like your financial plan, you should keep track of your budget and regularly review it. Focus on your expenses for every day of the month. You can write your budget on a spreadsheet or use an app to make it easy to track your expenses. In the next chapter, we will provide you with a list of various apps that can help you keep track of your finances.

Writing down all your expenses will help you recognize if you have unhealthy spending habits and will give you an idea if you are wasting your money on unnecessary items or not. Set a reminder on your phone so you remember to include the day's expenses in your budget every day. Don't wait until the end of the month because you will have forgotten what you spent your money on by then.

You should also set a spending limit for each of your expenses. However, as you are still new to budgeting, you may reach the spending limit before the end of the month. You will then be left with two options: accept that you have reached your limit, don't go over budget and make adjustments next month, or move money from another category, maybe from an unnecessary expense. For instance, if you eat out or order delivery food every day at work and run out of money, bring food from home instead, like sandwiches or a salad, instead of going over budget. Or you can use your transportation money to buy food and walk to work instead. The bottom line is that your expenses shouldn't exceed your income.

How to Save Money

Having a budget and sticking to it will help you save money. However, many people still struggle with saving. It's not easy, but it can get less complicated once you figure out how and can become a good habit to pick up.

Save Money from Your Salary Increases and Bonuses

Whenever we get a raise or a bonus at work, the first thing we do is spoil ourselves. You either buy something expensive you have always wanted, travel or go on a shopping spree. However, if you want to save or invest your money, your salary raise or bonus provides you with the perfect opportunity. So, when you get a raise, try not to change your spending habits. If you spend the same amount you did before your raise, the extra money can go to your savings account, retirement fund, or emergency fund.

You need to set money aside for emergencies, about three to six months' worth of expenses as we have mentioned. We suggest that you keep this money in a savings account where you can get a decent interest rate. You can take a percentage from it and add it to your savings account if you get a bonus. This will help you reach your goal of saving for an emergency fund faster. We suggest that you opt for a high-yield savings account because it is safe, offers interest over 2%, and you can easily withdraw your money whenever you need it.

How much money should you save each month? This mainly depends on your salary, financial situation, and expenses but finance experts suggest that you start saving 500$ each month and go up from there.

The Importance of an Emergency Fund

We have been stressing the importance of an emergency fund in the last chapter and this one, but what exactly is an emergency fund? Why is it so important?

What Is an Emergency Fund?

An emergency fund is taking a percentage of your salary and bonuses and putting them in a savings account in a bank. You only use this money in case of emergencies like losing your job, medical expenses, or major home or car repairs.

Why Is an Emergency Fund Important?

Losing Your Job

If you only depend on your salary for your income, then having an emergency fund is vital. It will serve as a safety net if you lose your job, especially if you have a family and are the sole breadwinner. Make sure to set a year's worth of expenses as your safety net to ensure you and your family are taken care of until you find a new job. Remember, you or a family member may suffer medical issues while you are out of work, so the larger your emergency fund, the better equipped you will be to handle these situations.

Unsteady Jobs

Whether your job or career is unsteady, like working as a freelancer or an artist, or self-employed with no unemployment benefits, you can benefit from an emergency fund. Self-employment isn't easy, and the market is unstable, some days up and others down. An emergency fund will keep you covered during the times when the market is down and your business is slow.

Medical Emergencies

Healthcare has become more expensive than ever. Many Americans suffer in silence because they can't afford to pay medical bills. A health issue can come out of nowhere, leaving you and your family struggling to make ends meet. You can't count on employer-sponsored insurance because you lose your insurance if you quit or were let go of your job. An emergency fund will help you give your family the best healthcare and provide you with peace of mind.

Another point to bear in mind is that if you or any family member suffer from chronic diseases or any health issues, this could leave you in debt. An emergency fund will keep you covered to pay for medication, hospital stay, and routine tests and check-ups.

Car and House Repairs

House and car repairs can be costly and are considered essential expenses if they are serious. For instance, if you use your car to drive to work every day, you will need to fix it right away rather than be late for work or have to pay for transportation. The same applies to your house; if your roof leaks or the water heater is broken, it will need to be fixed. As some of these problems can affect your lifestyle or the structure of the house, instead of stressing over these repairs or going into debt, you can simply dip into your emergency fund. However, your emergency fund is for emergencies only and not to be used for non-essential expenses like redecorating your house.

Helps You with Your Budget

Your emergency fund can help you with your budget. While you are planning your budget, there may be a few things that you forget to include. Having an emergency fund will help cover any unexpected expenses like gifts or fees while you are still in the first year of budgeting. An emergency fund will protect you from any surprises you haven't accounted for that can arise when you are on a budget.

Protect You from Debt

Being debt-free should be on your list of priorities of financial goals. Instead of borrowing money in the event of unexpected expenses, you can just tap into your emergency fund. You don't have to get into debt each time your car breaks down or a family member gets sick. Your emergency fund can cover all these expenses so you can remain debt-free.

Budgeting is an essential part of your financial plan, and it will help you achieve your financial goals and save money for the future. Sticking to your budget is vital as it is the only way to track your expenses and improve your spending habits. Consider budgeting and saving today, and you will notice your financial situation improving.

Chapter 5: Let Technology Help

No one becomes financially literate overnight. Since most people don't learn how to adjust their finances - for better or for worse - until well into their 20s, 30s, or even later, they realize that there's a lot of catching up they need to do. However, this is no reason to feel discouraged. Luckily, plenty of resources and apps can help you get your ducks in a row a lot faster than you think. The intersection between personal finances and technology has often been a cause of concern for many, and sometimes with good reason. With so much of our information online these days, it can be easy to fall prey to identity theft or scams. Yes, it can be scary, but you should be fine if you follow some basic protocols and are careful about the sites you trust. Now more than ever, technology isn't the enemy. In fact, when it comes to your finances, you should let technology help and do some of the work for you. This chapter will cover a few crucial techniques to help you make the most of the resources available to you to get closer to meeting your financial goals.

Tracking Expenses

There are a few key ways in which some technological tools can be used to help you track your expenses. Before you start, the first thing you need to do is figure out your spending habits by taking stock of all your accounts. Credit card companies and the vast majority of banks - maybe all of them, including smaller operations - will have an online portal that makes it easier to check your accounts. If you haven't signed up for the online portal, you should take the time to do so - it should only take a few minutes anyway. Then, you should have all of your accounts, including consumer debts and your mortgage, right at your fingertips. Looking at these accounts will help you precisely determine what you're spending and what. It will also spell out your cash flow situation, which is important.

So, now you have an easy-to-access snapshot of your financial reality. But you can't keep logging on from your desktop computer or laptop every day to continue keeping track. So, you'll need an easy way to keep up with your spending habits. Enter one of the first powerful tools available to you: online apps. You can look into different kinds depending on your own unique needs, so let's pause for a minute and figure out the kinds that may be most useful to you.

Online Banking

There are tools available in the online portals for your bank and credit cards that you should look into. The way to get the best out of these features is to get used to automating everything. For example, set up regular credit card payments to automatically deduct the money as soon as you get your check deposited. Also, set up automatic payments to a rainy day fund, your 401K, and the account you've set up for other things, like putting a down payment on a house. Even modest contributions will help; just make sure to get everything done automatically so that you don't overthink it as they say, out of sight, out of mind.

Apps that Can Help

In terms of apps, you should look at the ones specially designed to help you build a budget, which then will help inform your financial decisions. Sometimes, putting pen to paper to have a set budget in mind can be overwhelming, but apps can help take the guesswork out and will make it easier to manage your finances on the go. All you need to do is to input your information into an app - Mint - or the aptly named - You Need a Budget - are good places to start - and you will get an idea of what and how much to set aside every week or month. The old 30-20-10 rule - thirty percent living expenses, twenty percent fun, and ten percent savings - does not apply to every person. In fact, you may be able to set aside far more than ten percent in savings, which is preferable. Apps will help you do just that by letting you allocate a certain part of your income depending on what you need and what your debts look like. Furthermore, the apps can be synced to your bank accounts, so you will be able to know exactly what you're spending at all times, and you will be alerted right away if you fall into the trap of taking your account into overdraft.

Wondrous Excel

Ok, so most of us may hate spreadsheets or keeping track of our expenses in a google sheet. However, if you can't have apps work for you, you may need to reroute your efforts more effectively. Online spreadsheets are an excellent way of keeping track of your money, and there are plenty of free budget templates you can find online to help motivate you. They will make entering your expenses a lot clearer, and you can use the formulas in template sheets to determine the elements of your income you want to automatically set aside for other endeavors.

Alternatively, if you have a lot of complex finances to keep track of, you may purchase software online to help you. Quicken is a classic, and it lets you import all of your bank transactions in a sec while also helping you to monitor investments and other lines of debt you need to keep an eye on. Apps are excellent for some people, but others may benefit from the detail-oriented approach afforded by online sheets or software since it forces you to be more mindful while impressing upon you the importance of paying off debts sooner rather than later. Even better? Both software or any form of the sheet you use can be easily accessed on your phone or any portable device you carry, so financial investing is a breeze.

Benefits of Online Tracking

Online tracking has many clear benefits. While you can also keep a physical financial planner at the ready, that tactic doesn't work for everyone. A definite plus on the side of online tracking is that it makes it easy for you to check in on your accounts and spending immediately. Apps or software are always easy to access on any portable device you carry, not just your desktop, so you can cull the required information in a second. This helps to keep you far more accountable, which is necessary if you're still learning the basics of financial literacy. Or trying to undo the damage incurred by overzealous use of a credit card when you were a college student. You can set up warning messages on your phone to let you know straight away if you've overspent, if you are using money meant for a different savings account, and so on. Possessing that familiarity with your finances is necessary to help you exercise good habits and dispel any anxiety that comes with keeping on top of your money. Lots of people avoid looking at their online accounts for fear that they may see how far behind they are on meeting their goals. This, of course, is a self-defeating impulse since you can't meet your financial goals without knowing if your budgeting system is effective. Online tracking is one vital piece of the puzzle.

Best Budgeting Apps and Software

So, now we know the different ways in which technology can help you if you are amenable. Now you're probably wondering which apps and software to look into. The following is a quick list and review of the best tools available online and will provide the benefits and drawbacks of each one. You can decide which works best for you.

You Need a Budget

This was mentioned above, and it's really an excellent tool for newbies who need some guidance creating a feasible budget. If you have no idea where to start, then this is the tool for you.

Pros: Easy to import data, allows you to be flexible with shifting financial goals, and shows you how each dollar in your account will work to your benefit. Syncs with tens of thousands of banks, so you should be able to get things set up in just a few minutes. Not sure if it's the tool for you? There's a free one-month trial, which gives you a chance to assess the app.

Cons: The cost may be steep - nearly twelve dollars a month, which can be tough for people trying to climb out of debt to pay. Also, you can keep track of potential investments, and the app doesn't provide a general overview of your financial health. It really focuses on your need to create a budget and little else.

Mint

Another popular app that has already been mentioned here, Mint, has been increasing in popularity. It's one of the oldest budgeting apps on the market, and it has a loyal customer base. It's excellent for providing a general overview of your financial health and can help you assess where you need to go.

Pros: Easy and free to use, thus accounting for its popularity. You can also set it up to receive financial summaries and alerts via email or text, whichever works best for you. Also, you can easily obtain a copy of your credit score, which is essential in figuring out if you're doing ok financially or need to implement better spending habits.

Cons: You can't really use this app to invest. Furthermore, it doesn't always synchronize with the more niche bank accounts, so you may find yourself stranded in the cold. Users have also experienced trouble assigning more than one savings goal to one bank account, which isn't the best way to organize your finances. And free doesn't always mean convenient since you may receive more intrusive ads than you would like.

Lending Tree

You can access Lending Trees services via any web browser, but they also have a great app you could download. They're best known for being a viable referrer to loans while also helping you keep track of your credit score. It also tracks your spending and monitoring your net worth, which is extremely helpful.

Pros: Provides a complete overview of your financial outlook. It is also excellent in terms of functionality, and it allows you to monitor different areas of your financial realities, which other apps may not be able to do.

Cons: Some people in vulnerable financial situations may be pulled into the personal loan offers, which is not sound financial planning. While the loans tend to boast affordable interest rates, it's usually best to avoid these things since they may lure you into spending more than you can afford in the long run. Also, customers have reported receiving annoying telemarketing phone calls once they've shared their phone number with the app.

Quickbooks

This is the gold standard accounting software that has been readily available for individuals and businesses for decades. The software also comes with apps that you can easily download onto your phone or tablet to make the information easy to access.

Pros: Easy import of all invoices and banking details. Also, it allows you to keep track of investments, so it's a great motivator for people who are ready to move on to achieving more complex financial goals. Tracking of spending is straightforward to automate.

Cons: It is a bit more complex to use, so it may be better for people ready to move on to other financial goals. The subscription costs can be costly, and some individuals may feel that the process is too involved for personal financing.

Relying on technology to help make the process of becoming more confident with your financial literacy is a good move, especially for people new to the game. Apps and software can help you create an airtight budget with few vagaries that may be hard to miss when you use traditional pen and paper. Also, never underestimate the power of having so much of this work automated - it will take a huge load off your shoulders and help with any feelings of anxiety you may have when it comes to finances.

Chapter 6: Debts and Loans

At some point in life, we all face financial challenges that can prevent us from getting the things we want. Fortunately, if you need money to cover something that requires immediate attention, you can consider a loan or debt. You can use a loan within the agreed terms and conditions. When you decide to get credit, there are different things you should know.

This chapter explains what debt is and outlines the techniques to consider paying off your loans quickly. We also cover facts that potential borrowers should know about student loans. This chapter also covers pertinent things like helping the reader know how credit works and when and how to start paying off loans. Finally, we explain what bankruptcy is and when to consider it.

What Is Debt?

Debt refers to money borrowed by one party from the other with a promise of repaying it, usually with interest at a later date. Many people and corporations use debt to make big purchases that are not easy to afford using savings. A borrower approaches the lender, who in most cases is a registered financial institution like a bank, credit union, or any recognized entity.

Understanding Debt

Debt loan is mainly classified into four categories: secured, unsecured, mortgaged, and revolving. The most common types of debt include personal loans, payday loans, mortgages, credit card debt, student loans, auto loans, business loans, and others.

- **Secured Debt** - Secured debt requires collateral that is worth more than the money borrowed. If the borrower defaults on their re-payment obligation, the lender can repossess the asset used as collateral. Various assets are used as collateral, including houses, vehicles, boats, and investments.

- **Unsecured** - This type of debt is not secured by collateral. The debtor's ability to repay the loan is considered. However, this kind of debt usually comes with high interest since the debtors are often viewed as high risk. Unsecured debts include student loans and automobile loans. The amount of money you can get if you want this type of debt depends on income and employment status.

- **Revolving Debt** - This is a line of credit where you can borrow continuously as long as you pay back the funds owed. Credit card debt is a good example where borrowers continue to access debt from their providers.

- **Mortgages** - This is a special type of debt meant to purchase real estate like a house. This is a secured debt since the property purchased is used as collateral. If the borrower fails to repay their debt, they face the risk of foreclosure, where they lose the property and money.

Mortgage and student loans are probably the most popular types of loans since they are repaid over long periods ranging from 10 to 30 years. The terms and conditions of a loan stipulate that the borrower must repay the money owed by a certain date. The borrower should also pay interest as part of the credit terms.

Techniques to Pay Off Debt Quickly

When you seek a loan and get it, the next thing is to repay the money as agreed. Your lender stipulates the re-payment terms and conditions of your loan, and the onus is on you to pay it quickly. Late re-payments can lead to high interest and penalties that can seriously impact your financial situation. The following are some of the techniques you can use to pay off your loans.

Make Extra Payments

You can significantly save on interest by paying more than the required minimum payment every month. If you pay the extra money, it reduces the principal balance. However, you need to check if extra payments do not attract additional fees or penalties.

Another strategy you can consider is maintaining consistent payments on your credit card every month. Avoid late payments to prevent penalties and high interest. You can also lower your usage ratio by making regular payments.

Start with High-Interest Loan

If you have more debts, you should start your re-payments with the most expensive loan with a high-interest rate. When you pay this debt first, you decrease your overall debt and reduce interest. This is also known as the avalanche method, and it significantly lowers your overall costs on loan re-payment.

Alternatively, you can consider the debt snowball method, where you start by paying the smallest and then move to the largest debts. However, you should pay a minimum balance on any other debt you have. This will help you eliminate smaller loans and focus on the big picture.

Debt Refinancing

You can refinance your debt to a shorter term to pay it faster, and this will save you on the cost of borrowing. You will repay your debt at the same interest rate, but the life of your debt will become shorter. Similarly, loan consolidation is another level that helps you combine different loans with high-interest rates into a single loan with a lower interest rate. This method helps you focus on a single debt which lowers your monthly expenses. You can easily pay off your outstanding loans when you have more cash.

Reduce Monthly Bills

When you reduce your monthly bills, you will have more money which helps you repay your debts quickly. It is essential to stick to your budget and try to eliminate unnecessary expenses. For example, you can do away with monthly subscriptions that do not add value to your finances. When you lower your monthly costs, you will be able to make high installments on debt re-payment.

Earn Extra Cash

Try to look for a side hustle that will give you extra cash to repay your debts quickly. You can use your skills during your free time to generate additional income. You can consider a freelance gig to earn extra money while maintaining your daily schedule. Other activities like babysitting, dog walking, or online marketing jobs can give you additional money. Furthermore, you can sell unwanted items in your home like toys, jewelry, unused clothing, and books.

Things to Know about Student Loans

When you enroll in a college or university, you can apply for a student loan which you will use to cover your educational expenses. However, it is vital to understand the application process and re-payment terms associated with this kind of loan to make an informed decision. You can apply for a federal or private loan to fund your education. You need to consider the following factors when applying for a student loan.

Type of Loan

It is a good idea to choose a federal loan since it does not require credit history, it offers a flexible payment plan, and you can get loan forgiveness. If you get subsidized, it will not attract interest while still in school. However, a private loan does not offer all these benefits. You can only apply for a private loan when you fail to qualify for a federal loan.

When you apply for a student loan, make sure you get what you want to use. Applicants for both federal and private loans have a maximum amount they can get per year. This also determines the total amount they will get. You should use a student loan calculator to estimate your payments.

Interest and Fees

You should know that you pay fees and interest on your student loan. You must check the fees and interest rates to calculate the total amount you will need to repay. If you apply for a private loan, the lender will consider your credit history or your co-signers to determine the appropriate interest rate.

Your School Handles the Loan

When your loan is approved and you agree to the terms, the money is paid to the school. The students will only get leftover money to use on other expenses when the school has deducted the required funds for their education. You cannot use your student loan for other activities like vacations or anything unrelated to your education.

Make sure you use the money for transportation, personal supplies, and other education-related expenses. You may experience problems in paying back your loan if you are tempted to use it for other purposes. You also need to find out when to begin payments and get details about your servicer.

When and How to Start Paying Off Loans

Different types of loans come with various terms and conditions that include the re-payment period. For instance, federal student loans come with a grace period of six months after graduation before the commencement of re-payments. The grace period is meant to allow the graduates to look for work and settle first. Once the grace period is over, monthly payments should begin.

If you have a different type of loan, make sure you understand the terms and conditions before signing the agreement. If you are dealing with a private lender, they will require the borrowers to start repaying their loans beginning the following month. Private lenders are a bit strict, so make sure you make consistent and timely payments to avoid penalties and high interest. As explained in the section above, there are different measures you can take to repay your loan.

However, you can consider loan forgiveness if you cannot afford to repay your loan in full. The public service loan forgiveness facility is often extended to students working in the public service. After making specific payments working in this sector, the outstanding balance can be forgiven. If you don't qualify for loan forgiveness, try to talk to your employer or approach debt relief companies to see if they can assist you. However, if you are overwhelmed by debt and you feel there is no way you can raise the money within a certain period, you can consider the option of bankruptcy.

When to Consider Bankruptcy

When you feel that you cannot pay off your debts, the option of filing for bankruptcy can give you a fresh start while someone handles your debt payment. While there are several myths about declaring bankruptcy, it is a better decision that will give you financial relief in the long run. Remember, bankruptcy does not mean debt cancellation, but it's a way of making your life easier while managing your debts. The following are signs that should tell you when to consider bankruptcy.

Filing for bankruptcy can be tricky, so you must consider your goals and make an informed decision. You can consider filing for bankruptcy when you have outstanding bills but have exhausted all the avenues of getting money to pay them back. When you have tried other methods like loan negotiation or debt consolidation but failed, bankruptcy might be the only viable option.

When you realize that your house is at risk of foreclosure, you can consider filing for Chapter 13 bankruptcy. Instead of losing your house as a result of a mortgage that's past its due payment, Chapter 13

Bankruptcy allows you to keep specific assets. You can liaise with your lender and make a re-payment plan to pay off the debt while living in your home. Losing a home is not a pleasant prospect since you may not be able to buy another one.

You can also file for bankruptcy to protect your retirement savings since this will give you a fresh start while keeping your investment. Once you dip into your retirement savings to pay off debt, your future might be bleak since you may never be able to replace the retirement savings. Many people choose to protect their retirement investments and find other means of repaying their debts.

Unexpected incidents in life such as job loss, sudden illness, a worldwide pandemic, or the death of a family member can severely affect your finances. This will leave you in financial distress, affecting your loan re-payment. Filing for bankruptcy can be the most viable option to help you gain your footing while you take a mental step back and reconsider. However, you should consult a bankruptcy attorney or non-profit credit counselor before making this decision that can impact your life differently. Declaring bankruptcy can be traumatic, so you should handle it with care.

Types of Bankruptcy

When you are driven to choose the option of bankruptcy, you should make the best choice. There are mainly two types of consumer bankruptcy: Chapter 7 and Chapter 13. The main difference between these two options is that Chapter 7involves the total liquidation of your assets while Chapter 13 allows you to keep some or all of your belongings.

Chapter 7 Bankruptcy

When you file for Chapter 7 bankruptcy, all your non-exempt assets are liquidated to recover money to pay back your creditors. With this option, you lose everything, including your car, home, household possessions, and bank accounts. It is commonly known as fresh-start bankruptcy since it leaves you with just your clothes and a few ordinary goods.

Your creditors will get paid, and all your debts will be cleared. However, not everyone is eligible for Chapter 7 bankruptcy since the candidates who qualify should be earning below a specific level of income. It seems Chapter 7 is more common since many people file for bankruptcy under this option.

Chapter 13 Bankruptcy

Under Chapter 13, the debtor proposes a re-payment plan with the lender where they commit to paying everything due under a new agreement. This option is also referred to as re-payment bankruptcy. In most cases, a re-payment plan can take between 36 to 60 months to clear all your debts. By the time you complete your payments to the creditors, you will be clear of debt.

You can also make a payment plan with debt management companies who take over your debts and pay them over the agreed period. Chapter 13 bankruptcy allows you to keep most of your assets, but you must prove that you can make the payments under the proposed payment plan.

If you fail to maintain the terms and conditions set out in Chapter 13, you risk sliding to Chapter 7, where you will lose everything. Therefore, you must weigh the options available to make an informed decision. Whatever form of bankruptcy you choose, your debt remains in place. Filing for bankruptcy is just a way of removing the burden of dealing with debt collectors from you. It also allows you to start afresh when you have learned some important life lessons.

Loans are designed to give you financial relief when you hit hard times. You can get a loan when you want to make a big purchase that requires a significant amount of money you cannot raise. Whatever type of loan you get, make sure you should pay it back, and it is a good idea to pay it sooner to avoid penalties and high interests. There are several ways you can consider to manage your debt. However, if you cannot repay your debt over a certain period, you can consider bankruptcy as a last resort.

Chapter 7: Understanding Banks

When saving money, it's essential to understand how banks work. Choosing your bank and bank account type must be based on your financial needs, and after a thorough investigation of the instructions you decide to use. It is to make the most of the benefits these institutions offer you.

How to Identify the Right Bank

The first step you'll need to take is identifying the right bank for you. Here's what you need to know while doing so:

Understand the Types of Banks

There are three main types of banks you'll have to choose from:

- **Traditional Banks:** This is likely what you think of when you think of a bank. Traditional banks offer brick-and-mortar offices where they provide clients with banking and other financial services and have ATMs that people can use. They may offer online banking services as well.

- **Online Banks:** The popularity of online-only banks has grown massively over the years, partly due to their lower fees. The lower fees are a result of no overhead costs associated with physical branches, and these savings are passed on to clients. They are just as safe as other banks, but you will need to ensure that it is insured by the Federal Deposit Insurance Corp. or National Credit Union if you choose an online bank.

- **Credit Unions:** While traditional and online banks make a certain amount of profit off of your clientele, credit unions are not-for-profit financial cooperatives. They are member-owned, and members can avail of lower fees and higher interest rates. However, they usually have stricter rules for accessing services, and many don't offer online services, which can be a challenge if you need to access your bank account frequently.

We'll look at the pros and cons of each of these options further down the line.

Choose the Right Account

We'll go more into choosing the right account for your need further on in this chapter, but you need to know what type of account you're looking to open when choosing a bank. Deciding on an institution will do you no good if you visit and realize they do not allow you to open the type of bank account you want.

The other areas you need to consider are their options for debit and credit cards, especially if you prefer going cashless when possible. You should also look at what lending products they offer. This includes things like mortgages and personal loans – while you may not need to borrow money at the moment, it's always best to understand your options in case you need to do so in the future.

Look at Fees

Ideally, the bank you choose should charge little to no fees. After all, you're at a bank to save money, not spend it!

Credit unions and online banks are the best options for low fees, as mentioned above. However, some traditional banks are also taking steps to reduce fees, so keep all your options open.

Some major fees to keep an eye on include monthly maintenance fees, overdraft fees, and ATM fees. Overdraft fees are the most challenging – these are essentially the fees that your bank charges you every time you use their automatic overdraft service. The overdraft service is when you withdraw more money from your account than what you currently have in it, similar to taking a small loan from the bank.

This means an unnecessary expense and can have an extremely significant effect on your budget depending on the bank in question and how much "extra money" you withdrew. Because of the financial burden that the overdraft fee cause, many banks have taken the step to eliminate it altogether, so make sure to check on this when choosing a bank.

You should also look at taking steps to reduce additional fees, including:

- Linking your checking account to another account at the bank. This means if you do overdraw from the checking account, the money is covered by your second account, and you don't have to worry about overdraft fees. This is also known as overdraft protection.

- Sign up for bank alerts that warn you when you're at risk of overdrawing from your account.

- Ask your bank if there is a way to waive the monthly maintenance fees. Banks generally require you to have a minimum balance or set up your direct deposits if you want this fee to be waived.

Keep the Pros of a Traditional Bank Branch in Mind

As mentioned above, traditional banks generally have the highest fees of your three options. However, there are several benefits that a physical bank branch offers you that you will not be able to find with an online bank.

Physical branches are a great option for people who aren't familiar with the ins and outs of banking and may require help getting their feet under them. With the option of a physical location, you can easily walk in and ask someone for help. While online banks generally have a robust customer service team, it often doesn't make up for in-person interaction, and many people find online or phone-based customer service frustrating.

Traditional banks also offer ATM services, which can be essential for many people. However, bank ATMs can also be accessed by customers of other banks, so if you choose an online bank, you may still be able to use the ATM machines operated by your local traditional bank.

If you do decide that a traditional bank is right for you, there are a number of convenience factors you should keep in mind when deciding on a specific bank. Some considerations include:

- Whether they offer online and mobile banking services

- Where their physical branch is located, and how accessible it is for you

- Where their ATMs are located, and how convenient those locations are for you

Which of these you should value the most depends on your needs. For example, if you prefer doing all your banking in person, you may focus more on the location of their physical branch. However, if you prefer online banking and choose a traditional bank for reasons other than in-person customer service, you may prefer to focus ontheir online banking services.

Consider Credit Unions

As discussed above, credit unions are a good alternative to banks – they offer the low fees associated with online banks with the in-person convenience of traditional banks. However, keep in mind that you need to be a member of the credit union in question before opening a bank account with them.

Joining credit unions is easier than it ever has been. However, there may not be a credit union you qualify for located near your home, so make sure to research your local options. Some credit unions require you to be part of a certain subsection of people. For example, the Navy Federal Credit Union is limited to military service members and their families. The American Airlines Federal Credit Union is limited to airline industry employees and family members.

That said, it should be possible to find at least one credit union you're eligible for near you, especially if you live in a major city. Several are available across the country, and some allow you to qualify for membership by doing something as simple as donating to a related charitable organization. So, if you're interested in a credit union, make sure to take a thorough look at your options.

Make Sure the Bank You Choose Can Support Your Needs

The bank you choose should be able to support you over the years, and not just at present. For example, if you're trying to save money, look for banks that offer high yield savings accounts and the ability to open and name separate savings accounts (for example, one account for retirement, one for travel, etc.). Ideally, you'll be staying with this bank for the long term, so you don't want to be caught by surprise years down the line.

Consider Their Digital Offerings

While most banks today have a website and likely a basic app that allows you to transfer funds, pay bills, and complete other essential actions, not all offer more advanced capabilities. Make sure to consider what digital offerings a bank offers before making a decision and whether you need those offerings.

For example, if you don't plan on applying for a debit card, you probably won't worry about whether your bank will let you lock it and prevent strangers from using it. On the other hand, people who prefer online banking will likely prefer a bank that offers a smartphone app instead of only a desktop portal.

Read the Terms and Conditions

We know that the terms and conditions of any contract are the most boring part – and while you may be tempted to overlook them, you must read them all in detail. There's a lot of important information hiding in the account agreement that you may not find elsewhere on the bank's website, and you can also make sure you're not committing to any hidden fees.

Additionally, the terms and conditions usually include things like:

- Situations in which monthly maintenance fees will be waived

- What out-of-network ATM charges you will incur if you use another bank's ATM

- Whether the bank is federally insured so that you don't lose out if it closes

- When promotional deals expire.

This information will come in handy in the long term and can even prevent you from choosing the wrong bank.

Read Reviews

You can do all the research in the world, but that won't make up for hearing the unvarnished truth from other customers. Seek out online reviews and speak to friends and family who may have experience with the bank you're considering. They can often clue you into things you won't realize at first glance, such as how their customer service is and any challenges you may have to overcome in the future.

What about Online Banking?

We've discussed keeping the possibility of online banking in your mind when choosing a bank – but what exactly is online banking, and why is it so popular?

Online banking is essentially what it sounds like – the ability to make financial transactions via the Internet. It can offer nearly every service you'd get from a traditional bank, including online bill payments, deposits, transfers, and more. However, each bank offers different online banking options, so yours may not offer all the options mentioned above.

So, why is it so popular? After all, most people have grown up hearing the dangers of sharing your personal information online – and your bank details are some of the most private pieces of information about your life. If they get out, there are significant privacy concerns you'll have to contend with.

While this is true, banks offer safe, secure online bank platforms that will keep your information private. Of course, you'll need to be alert and take common-sense measures such as keeping your passwords secret. However, in general, it's actually a rather safe undertaking.

Online banking is popular for multiple reasons, one of the major ones being the convenience it offers. You do not have to make your way to a brick-and-mortar location and can complete transactions from the comfort of your own home. This also means you have to earmark less time for banking, allowing you greater time in your day for other pursuits.

Additionally, it's fast and efficient, and funds can be transferred between accounts and institutions almost instantly. You can open and close accounts online without interacting with other people if you prefer not to.

Most institutions allow customers to monitor and access their accounts around the clock, allowing you to ensure your accounts are safe. This also allows you to detect fraudulent activity quickly, reducing the possible harm to your financial health.

Finally, you have greater access to your bank records, allowing you to download and print them as needed. You no longer have to make the trip to your branch in person and wait for a staff member to do it for you – you'll have what you need in minutes, allowing you to complete tax fillings quicker.

The Different Types of Bank Accounts

As mentioned above, we'll now take a look at the different types of bank accounts you can choose from. Which one you choose will depend on your unique financial needs.

Checking Accounts

A checking account is for money that you'll be accessing frequently or on a daily basis. This is the account from which you will draw the money you spend on groceries, rent, and other similar expenses.

For this reason, they're also the most accessible type of bank account and generally have few or no limits when it comes to deposits and withdrawals.

These accounts generally do not earn interest, but some banks and credit unions may offer interest-bearing checking accounts. They usually come with a debit card.

Savings Accounts

These are exactly what they sound like – accounts designed to save money that you won't be spending immediately. You earn interest on the money saved in these accounts, and they are the right option for long-term emergency funds and goals like buying a home.

Savings accounts often have some restrictions on how frequently you can withdraw or transfer money from them and generally don't come with a credit or debit card.

Money Market Accounts

Money market accounts (MMAs) are essentially a combination of savings and checking accounts. They have a higher interest rate than savings accounts but also often have higher minimum balance rules. Additionally, the number of withdrawals is usually limited. However, some MMAs come with credit/debit cards. They're a good option if you have a high balance that you're looking to save and earn interest on.

Certificates of Deposit

Also known as CDs, these accounts help you invest money at a fixed interest rate for a fixed period of time. There is minimal risk involved with this account versus many other investment products. Terms vary depending on the bank and the account and range from months to years.

You must commit to keeping the money in the account for the entire term, and in return, you're promised a higher interest rate than other accounts offer. You can incur a high withdrawal penalty if you need to withdraw money early (though some banks offer CDs with lower interest rates and no-penalty withdrawals). If you're sure you won't need to access the money for the specified period, CDs are a good way to grow your money passively.

Most banks offer variations on these four main types of accounts – interest rates and minimum balances will differ from bank to bank and account to account. Once you've decided on which type of account and which bank to use, you can then ask about what options they have available under your preferred account type.

Understanding Interest Rates

We've discussed interest on bank accounts a lot, but you may find yourself wondering – what is interest? Why would you earn it on a savings account?

The interest you earn on your bank account (usually savings accounts, MMAs, or CDs) is essentially the money your bank gives you for storing your money in that bank. This is paid as a percentage of your balance – so, if your bank account offers a 1% interest rate, you'll earn more if you have $100,000 in your savings account than if you have $10,000.

The interest is paid to you because a bank essentially "borrows" the money you store with them to finance loans given to other customers. When you take out a loan, you must repay it with interest. A portion of that interest is paid out to you in your bank account.

This is also why a checking account does not usually pay out interest. Because you will frequently be accessing the money in that account, your bank cannot lend it out to other customers – and so cannot pay you interest on the money in that account.

Interest earned on savings accounts is compounded. Consider a situation in which you have a 10% annual interest rate on an initial savings account of $1000. (Keep in mind that real interest rates are significantly lower than 10% - this is purely offered as an example).

In the first year, you will earn 10% of $1000 – which is to say, $100. This interest (unless withdrawn) will be retained in your bank account, and you will have a new account balance of $1100.

You will earn another 10% as interest on your bank account in year two. However, you will now make 10% on $1100 – which is $110. So, you're earning more money as interest as you did in year one.

In this way, you can earn quite a bit over a long period of time on a savings account, which can help you grow an emergency fund. This is why it's generally recommended you ask around at different banks to see which offers the best interest rates.

Keep in mind that just because a bank offers high-interest rates, it doesn't mean it's the right option for you. Some banks offer higher interest rates due to other failures in their institution, such as lack of federal insurance, bad customer service, and risk of failure. Make sure you research a bank thoroughly before choosing it to look after your money.

Banks can be complex institutions to navigate, especially if you don't have any prior experience with them. However, as long as you do your due diligence, you'll soon realize that they're not as incomprehensible as they seem.

If you have any further questions or find that you have difficulties navigating the banking system, don't hesitate to reach out to a staff member at your bank for help. They'll be able to understand your financial needs in-depth and guide you regarding which account is best for you.

Additionally, always remember that you are not limited to one bank - you can also open accounts in different banks. This is often seen as a strategy that allows individuals to hedge their bets and ensures you don't put all your eggs in the same basket. Furthermore, while one bank may offer the perfect checking account, another may be better for your savings needs. By keeping all your options open, you can make the best of both worlds.

Chapter 8: Credit Cards

You have heard about credit cards and debit cards, but some misconceptions are often associated with them. This chapter will explain the difference between a credit card and a debit card. We will also explain the time value of money and why it is important to understand it. We also discuss credit card myths and everything you may want to know about credit cards, including their dangers.

What Is the Difference between a Credit and Debit Card?

Credit cards and debit cards share several similarities like 16-digit card numbers, magnetic strips, expiration dates, and EMV chips. Both are convenient and easy to use, but they come with important differences that can impact your financial situation.

A credit card is offered by a specific financial institution like a bank, and it allows the holder to borrow money from the institution. When you apply for a credit card, you agree to repay the money borrowed interest. In other words, a credit card works like a loan facility where you borrow some money to purchase different products and services.

On the other hand, a debit card is issued by your bank, and it is linked to your checking account. When you use this card to purchase products or services, you are using the money you already have in your account. There is no interest in using your debit card since you will be buying different things with your money. The only difference is that credit card is plastic money. When no money is available in your account, you cannot use your debit card to buy goods.

Credit cards belong to different categories that include the following:

- **Standard Cards** – Provide a line of credit to the users for cash advances, balance transfers, or making purchases. They have no annual fee.

- **Premium Cards** – Offer various perks like airport lounge access, concierge services, and special event access, and they come with higher annual fees.

- **Reward Cards** - Provide travel points, cash back, and other benefits depending on usage of your card

- **Secured Credit Cards** – You pay an initial deposit that acts as collateral.

- **Balance Transfer Cards** - Have low fees when transferring balances to another card.

Benefits of Using a Credit Card

You can get many benefits from using credit cards, such as discounts, cash, and travel points. You can use your credit card to get discounts on your flight bookings. The following are some of the advantages of using a credit card.

- **Build Credit History** - You can use your credit card to build your credit history as all transactions appear on your credit statement. Timely payments contribute to a positive credit score, while late payments negatively impact it.

- **Warranty and Purchase Protections** - If you buy a product whose manufacturer's warranty has expired, your credit card company can provide coverage.

- **Fraud Protection** - Credit card companies offer fraud protection, and the maximum liability of purchases conducted after the loss or theft of the credit card has been reported is $50. Credit card users can dispute goods that are damaged during shipping.

Disadvantages of Using Credit Cards

The main disadvantage of using a credit card is that it can so easily lead to a cycle of debt. When you use your credit card, you spend the bank's money, not yours. This money will need to be repaid with a good dollop of interest, and you'll have to make a minimum payment every month. If you have multiple balances on different cards, it can strain your brain to remember each one, not only your budget, and you may fail to keep pace with your monthly budget. Late payments can affect your credit history. Furthermore, credit card usage comes with interest and fees since this is a form of short-term loan. The interests and fees vary depending on the financial institution involved.

What Is a Debit Card?

A debit card can be used for making payments by deducting money from your checking account. You must have a savings or checking account to get a debit card. The following are the common types of debit cards.

- Standard debit card- linked to your bank account.

- Electronic benefits transfer cards- state or federal agencies issue these to users who qualify to use their benefits for making a purchase.

- Prepaid debit card- issued to people without bank accounts.

Many people prefer to use debit cards to eliminate the danger of building up huge credit. With this card, you will be using your money, so there is no way you can rack credit. Debit cards issued by Visa or Mastercard offer fraud protection, giving you peace of mind. Debit cards don't have annual fees, and you will not be charged for withdrawing your money from the ATM.

You cannot earn rewards for using your credit card. Your debit card does not help build a good credit score. Debit cards come with fees, such as using foreign ATMs. You don't earn rewards for using your debit card.

Credit Card Myths

There are several myths associated with credit cards, and some of them make people skeptical about using these cards. While some myths hold some kind of truth, others are false. The following are some things you should know about credit cards before getting one.

You Must Keep a Balance on Your Credit Card

Many people believe that you must have a balance on your credit card if you want to build your credit. Instead, carrying a balance on your credit card can attract interest. However, you should pay off your credit balance in full every month if you can. Make all payments before the statement date to maintain a clean record and avoid interest costs.

It's Best to Close the Card After Paying It Off

Closing your credit card after paying it off can damage your credit. This can lead to the shortening of your credit history, impacting your credit score. You can keep it active by making small subscriptions.

High Credit Is Bad

Another myth is that a high credit limit is bad, but the opposite is true. If you have self-control and you can manage all your monthly payments, there is nothing wrong with using a credit card. You should try to keep your usage lower and make sure you spend money you can afford to repay each month.

Credit Score Increases By Spending More

Some people have a misconception of believing that spending more can lead to a rise in the credit score. However, the truth is that credit usage and regular payments determine your credit score. Your credit score is not related to how much you spend but the way you use your credit.

You Can Lower Your Credit Score By Checking It

Another myth is that checking your credit score can lower it. The truth is that it is a good thing to monitor your credit. Hard inquiries will go to your credit history, and soft inquiries will not affect it. You can use your bank or credit card app to check your credit score in real-time, and this is regarded as a soft inquiry. It does not damage your credit. Checking your credit reports shows that you are responsible, but you must not overdo it.

You Must Pay the Minimum Due Amount

Some people believe that you must only pay the minimum due amount on your credit card each month. But, if possible, try to pay as much as you can, although it is okay to make the minimum payments required by the credit card issuer. However, interest charges will continue to build, so paying more is better.

Maintain Your Credit Card Usage at 30 Percent

Some people believe that your credit card usage should be maintained at 30 percent to create good credit. The truth is that you should not exceed 30% of the limit on your credit. Keeping it at zero is the best method that can help you avoid paying high credit card interest rates. Your payment history is the most important factor that determines your credit history. You must avoid late payments if you want to build a good credit score.

One Credit Card Is Enough

Although some people believe that one credit card is enough, you may need other credit cards since they bring other perks and benefits. As long as you exercise financial discipline, there is nothing wrong with having more than two credit cards. Other credit cards offer the best rates for international travel bookings. When you apply for a credit card, you should know its benefits to make an informed decision. Feel free to check with the credit company to get the best card that suits your needs.

What Is Credit Score, and How to Keep It Stable

A good credit score is vital to qualify for the best mortgage, credit card, and competitive loan rates. A credit score is measured from 300 to 850, and it is used to determine your eligibility to get a loan. Your credit score tells the lender about your ability to repay your credit and potential credit risk.

There are mainly two methods of measuring credit scores: FICO and Vantage Score. In the US, FICO is commonly used to measure your score. Credit scores are divided into the following ranges by FICO.

- 300 to 579: very poor
- 580 to 669: fair
- 670 to 739: good
- 740 to 799: Very good
- 800 to 850 Excellent

On the other hand, vantage scores are measured according to the following ranges.

- 300 to 499: very poor
- 500 to 600: poor
- 601 to 660: fair
- 661 to 780: good
- 781 to 850: excellent

If you have a poor credit score, you may not qualify to get credit since you will pose more risk to the lenders. You may be charged high interest if you qualify to get a loan with a low credit score.

Building Credit Score

When you have bad credit, there are different measures you can take to improve it. The following are some of the aspects you should prioritize.

- **Make Timely Payments** – Your payment history is the most critical factor determining your credit score. Make sure you pay all your bills and credits on time to improve your rating. You can set auto-pay for smaller credits.

- **Pay in Full** - To reduce your credit utilization rate, you should meet your minimum payment requirements.

- **Avoid Opening Several Credit Accounts** - Whenever you apply for credit, an inquiry appears on your report whether the loan is approved or denied. Your credit score will be affected by about five points, which can impact your score, although it is temporary. Maintaining several lines of credit can pose some challenges in the long run.

If you have a good credit score, you can qualify for a mortgage, car loan, or other forms of credit. It also helps you get the best APRs from lenders. A good credit score also helps you get the best credit card with many benefits like rewards and discounts. However, credit card issuers also consider other elements like your monthly income and other credits you have.

Understanding Time Value for Money

The time value of money (TVM) is an essential tool that helps you understand the worthiness of money compared to the value of time in any kind of investment. The basic underlying principle of the TVM concept is that money has more value in its present form than in the future since it can be affected by elements like inflation. For instance, $1,000 can buy you more things today than you would get with the same amount 10 years from now.

The TVM concept helps you make an informed decision when you invest your money, considering that its value changes. You are likely to encounter some risks when you invest in a business. Therefore, you will choose the best investment option when you understand the inflation, interest, risk, and return elements. If you find a good investment option that gives you healthy interest, it can be a good idea to consider it since it will give you more money in return.

The Danger of Credit Cards

A credit card offers many benefits, but it can be potentially dangerous. If you are a new credit card user, you can easily fall into traps like believing the promises offered. If you intend to get a credit card, you should know the dangers associated with these cards. The following are some of the dangers you should know about credit cards so you can use them responsibly.

Avoid the Temptation to Overspend

Many people often spend more when they use credit cards than when they pay with cash. When you buy with a credit card, you don't feel the pain as what you do with cash. The bad part about a credit card is that you will be using the money you don't have. You can buy using cash to avoid this challenge. Additionally, make an effort to pay your balance in full.

Risk of Getting into a Debt Trap

Whenever you borrow money, you will be creating debt. If you continue to borrow without paying, you will create a debt trap, leading to a myriad of other challenges you can encounter. Debt leads to health-related problems such as depression, stress, and other conditions that can seriously impact your wellbeing.

It can be difficult to realize other financial goals when you are overwhelmed by debt. When you spend more money on debt repayment, you will be left with little cash for other priorities such as saving for retirement plans. You can also delay other goals like pursuing your studies when you are debt-ridden.

When you realize that you are failing to pay your credit card balance in full every month, you should stop using your credit card. Instead, use cash and try to live within your budget to avoid ruining your financial situation.

Risk of Damaging Your Credit Score

If you miss your monthly credit card payments, your credit score will slide, and you may not be able to get a loan in the future. You also risk ruining your credit score if you fail to exercise discipline with your credit card. The best way to avoid this situation is to maintain your balance below 30% of the credit limit, pay your balance on time, and minimize the number of credit cards you have at any given time.

Minimum Payments Can Give You a False Impression

Your credit card requires you to make minimum monthly payments to avoid late fees and maintain your account in good books. However, there is a danger that this can give you a false sense of security since your balance will remain even if you maintain minimum payments. This will also attract more interest, so you will not be doing any good by paying minimum interest. It is a good idea to pay your balance in full if you can. If you cannot afford to pay in full, try to pay more than the minimum balance required by the lender. This will help you reduce the interest on your balance.

Credit Card Terms Can Be Confusing

Credit card terms and conditions can be confusing, impacting your repayment plan. There are serious consequences for misunderstanding the terms and conditions of your credit card. A single credit card can come with different interest rates, and you may not know the right ones to use. This can lead to increased interest rates and fees. You should read between the lines to understand the types of balances and interest rates each credit card carries. It is vital to consult your credit card issuer's customer service to get all the details you may want about your credit card.

It Is Difficult to Track Spending on Several Credit Cards

It can be difficult to track your spending when you have several cards, affecting your repayment plan. If you use your credit cards together with cash and debit cards, it will be difficult to monitor your spending. As a result, you may overspend because you will be out of touch with your finances.

You should use different methods to track the expenses on your credit cards. For instance, you can track your spending manually or use special software. Check all credit card statements and report any suspicious activity to your credit card issuer.

Credit Card Fraud

Credit card fraud is common, and it can lead to financial loss. There is a risk of losing your credit card or your personal information can be stolen. If you lose your card, you should quickly make a report to your credit card company. It is essential to monitor your credit card closely, and you should not share it with anyone.

High-Interest Rate

If you fail to pay your credit balance in full every month, there is a danger that interests will add up quickly. The interest charged by the issuer depends on the type of credit card you have. Choosing the best credit card that suits your needs is crucial to avoid issues like high interest. You also need to strive to pay your monthly balance in full to avoid high interests and fees. If you cannot pay the full amount, make sure you pay more than the minimum amount required. You also need to exercise financial discipline when you use your credit card.

While credit and debit cards share many similarities, they are very different. A credit card provides a line of credit from the issuer, and it comes with interest, whereas a debit card is linked to your savings or checking account. If you want to maintain your finances in good order, a debit card is your perfect fit. If you are concerned about cashing rewards and building your credit score, you can consider a credit card. No matter which option you choose, you should know the benefits and downsides of each.

Chapter 9: Investing

Many people often face challenges in managing their finances, but this should not be a problem when you have the right knowledge. This chapter will discuss different techniques you can use to manage your money. We will also explain the meaning of investing and highlight the steps you can take. In the last part, we discuss different investment options.

How to Manage Your Money

You can take different steps to manage your money to avoid issues like overspending. You can track your expenses and make meaningful investments with proper financial management. The following are some steps you can take to manage your finances.

Track Your Spending

To improve your finances, you should track your spending to know where your money is going every month. You can do this by keeping your receipts or recording all your expenditures. You can make your life easy by using a money management app to track spending in different categories in this digital era. This will help you gain insight into the total amount you spend on non-essential things like entertainment and eating out. When you know how your money is wasted, you can make a better plan to improve your finances.

Create a Monthly Budget

Budgeting is one of the most important things that help you manage your money. After tracking all your expenses, you should create a realistic budget to allocate your money toward pertinent things you require in your daily life. However, remember to create a flexible budget that suits your lifestyle and spending habits.

Your budget should be realistic, and it is a way of encouraging you to practice better habits in spending your money. However, there is no need to create a strict budget or punish yourself since you are entitled to enjoy the benefits of your hard work. You only need to make sure your budget is flexible and avoid spending the money you don't have. You should prioritize basic things in your budget to avoid straining your financial resources.

Save Your Money

You should learn to build your savings, and you can achieve this by creating an emergency fund you can turn to when you experience an emergency. Don't worry about the money you save per month. Even if it is little, it can make a difference. One day it will save you from a risky situation that can force you to apply for a loan that usually comes with high interest.

At some point in time, getting a loan is inevitable, but you would rather consider other better options first. With general savings, you can strengthen your financial security. Automated savings can help you contribute to the emergence fund without fail.

Pay Your Bills on Time

You should always make sure you pay all your bills on time so that you do not ruin your credit history. It might be difficult for you to get a loan to purchase other items you cannot buy using your savings with a poor credit score. Additionally, you also have late fees and high interests when you make timely payments. This can go a long way in helping you save your monthly earnings.

You can also save your money by cutting back on recurring charges that you can do away with. For instance, you can cancel all unnecessary subscriptions to streaming services or other mobile apps that you rarely use.

Use Cash

When you buy consumer products like groceries and other smaller items, it is better to use cash instead of your credit card. You should know about credit card use because it is a short-term loan that should be paid back at the end of the month. A credit card also generates interest that can haunt you for several years, leading to the creation of a debt cycle. However, you can avoid hype buying when you use cash. This method only allows you to use the money you have, unlike when you buy with a credit card.

Start Investing Today

One of the most effective methods to manage your money is to start an investment that will help you generate more income. If you properly manage your finances, you can end up with more money. We will discuss different things you should know about investing your money in the next section.

What Is an Investment?

Investing is the process of buying assets or performing any activity that can increase the value of your money in the future, where you can get returns in the form of capital gains or income payments. Even when you are no longer going to work, you can enjoy passive income continuously from your investment. It is all about spending your money and time to improve your welfare in the long run.

There are different investment vehicles you can consider, and these are designed to help you earn additional income or a profit from your initial deposit. However, investment comes with risks and losses, so not all investments are profitable. You should know different things before investing your money so you make an informed decision.

How to Start Investing

There are several forms of investment options to consider depending on your long-term goals. Here are some tips that can guide you in your investment journey.

Pick an Investment Strategy

The first thing you should do is to pick a strategy determined by the amount you want to invest and the timeline for your investment. Other investment firms are simple, and you can start with little money. You can also opt out whenever you want, especially when you choose short-term investments.

However, other investments require large sums of money, which are long-term. You should also know the amount of risk posed by each type of investment vehicle you choose.

Start Investing Early

If you want to make a long-term investment, it is vital to get started early. When you invest when you are still young, your money will get enough time to grow. Remember, your money will gain interest to choose the ideal timeline that suits your needs.

If you invest more money, it means you will get handsome returns at the end of your investment term. For instance, if you make monthly contributions of $200 for 10 years at an average annual interest of 6% of your investment, you will get $33,000 at the end of the investment period. Your total contributions would be $22,400, while $9,100 will be your interest.

While the market has ups and downs, long-term investment can benefit you more. If you don't invest your money and choose to keep it in your savings account, there is a risk that it can be eroded by inflation.

Decide How Much You Want to Invest

Your investment goal should determine the total amount of money you can invest. Suppose retirement is a common goal of an investment. In that case, you must use a retirement calculator to try to figure out the total income you can get from your investment after a particular period. Again, it will be easier if you start your retirement plan when you are still active and fully employed.

Choose an Investment Account

You can invest for retirement using the usual 401(k) or use an individual account such as a traditional or Roth IRA. However, if you have another investment goal different from retirement, you should pick an appropriate account that suits your needs. A taxable brokerage account is a perfect option since it allows you to withdraw your money anytime you need it.

Another thing about opening an investment account is that you don't need large sums of money to get one. You can invest as little as $500 and still get an account of your choice. It is vital to do your research first to identify an investment that requires a relatively small amount of money.

Understand the Fees Charged By Brokers

To succeed in your investment, make sure you know the minimum deposit required to start your investment. You should also understand how the market operates to avoid losing your money. You should not be tempted to venture into any form of investment you are not familiar with since this can lead to losses.

You must go through customer reviews to gain insight into what other people say about the brokerage before opening an account. The good thing about customer reviews is that they are objective, and you will learn different things from them like account management fees, minimum deposits, trading fees, and other aspects that can affect your trade.

Commission and fees are other essential elements you should know since they can impact your total earnings. You need to know that brokers make their money from the clients, but check if the commissions charged are reasonable. Every time you trade, your broker will charge a commission for using their platform. While other brokers do not charge a commission, they will recover the money somehow. There is nothing like free lunch or charitable work.

Key Takeaways to Succeed in Your Investment

If you do your research well, you will likely succeed in your investment. Just make sure you keep the following tips in mind to achieve your goals.

- Aim for a long term investment

- Investments with better potential rewards come with higher risks and losses.

- If you are new to investment, you can consider investing in funds, not stocks.

- You should diversify your investment to reduce the impact of severe losses if one investment fails.

- You should read widely to understand the market forces that can impact your investment.

Different Investing Options

There are different investment options you can consider. The following are the common types of investment preferred by different people.

Invest in Stocks

When you invest in stocks, you buy shares in public companies, and you do this in anticipation of earning dividends when the company grows. Your shares will become valuable when the company improves its performance. You can also sell your stocks to other investors, giving you a profit.

Stocks are also known as equities, and they can be purchased for thousands of dollars. When you buy stocks, you will be included in the company's profit-sharing. When the company performs well, you will also get more revenue depending on the available stocks. It is a good idea to purchase stocks through a mutual fund. You can put your money in an online investment account, and it is used to purchase stocks.

Get as much information as possible about the kind of trade you want to undertake so you don't make losses. If you want to invest in stocks, you should first practice trading with market simulators before using real money. This will help you determine if the kind of trade you want to venture into is your perfect fit.

Investing through Your Employer

You can invest part of your salary through your employer's investment plan. You can ask your employer to add you to the scheme if money for your pension contributions is not automatically deducted from your salary.

If you invest using your employer's 401 (k), you will not miss any contribution, and your money will start to accumulate at an early stage. By the time you reach retirement age, you will have a substantial amount of money. Making small contributions over a long period is a great way of adding value to your money since you can get a lump sum when you finally retire and monthly payments.

Bonds

You can also invest in bonds, but this method requires substantial money before you get started. A bond is a special type of loan to a government, company, or municipality which agrees to pay you back over a certain period. When you choose this investment, you will get your interest first. Bonds are mainly used for large construction projects or other bigger tasks like infrastructural development.

The main advantage of bonds is that they are less risky than other options like stocks that can be unpredictable. With a bond, you know the amount of money you will get and the time you should be paid back. However, bonds don't earn better returns in the long run. Therefore, bonds should constitute a smaller segment of your investment portfolio. You cannot solely rely on bonds since they will not give you enough money to sustain you in the long run.

Mutual Funds

Mutual funds consist of different forms of investments combined. When you choose to invest in mutual funds, you will skip the hassle of selecting bonds and stocks. Instead, you can buy a collection of investments in one transaction. Mutual funds are diversified, making them less risky compared to other investments like stocks that can be volatile.

Professionals often manage mutual funds, but some of them are determined by the performance of a certain market index. This means the index can offer lower fees due to the elimination of professional funds. You should understand the difference between mutual funds and index funds to make an informed decision in your investment.

Exchange-Traded Funds

Exchange-traded funds (EFTs) are perfect for people who are still new to the stock market. The main benefit of this option is that EFTs are cheap, and they come with lower risk compared to individual stocks. The main reason is that a single fund consists of a collection of a variety of investments. If you want to diversify your investment portfolio, you can consider ETFs.

Another aspect of EFTs is that they trade throughout the day, and their price is often lower than the requirement for investing in a mutual fund. To sell ETFs, you should have a brokerage account, and all forms of trade would be done online. Most brokerages don't have transaction or inactivity fees, and they have no account minimums. Opening a brokerage account is a simple process not very different from opening a bank account.

If you want someone to handle your investment on your behalf, you should get an account with a Robo-advisor. They will build and manage your investment, and you will be charged a relatively low annual fee. However, you need to monitor your account regularly.

Commodities

Commodities include different things like precious metals, energy products, and agricultural products. These are usually raw materials used in various industries, and their prices are determined by market demand. For instance, the scarcity of particular agricultural products can lead to an increase in their price.

When you invest in commodities, it does not necessarily mean that you will hold them physically. Most investors buy commodities using options and futures contracts or via securities such as ETFs. The other option of investing in commodities is buying shares from the companies that offer them. When you become a shareholder, you will be included in the profit-sharing.

The danger of investing in commodities is that they come with relatively high risks. Investing in options and futures mainly depends on the money you borrow, which can lead to unprecedented losses if the market for commodities performs below expectations. The other risk of investing in commodities is that their price is determined by several factors beyond the control of many people. However, gold is a good investment since it is viewed as a storage of value.

Real Estate

Investing in the real estate sector is one of the wisest decisions you can make if you want to enjoy passive income in your entire lifetime. The good thing about investing in properties is that their value appreciates over time, so you are always assured of better returns in whatever type of investment you choose.

For instance, you can invest in buying and selling homes or other properties. You can buy a property and sell it later when the price increases. However, you need to upgrade the house first so that it can fetch a high price when you sell it. This will help you generate handsome properties. You can also consider investing in rental properties. These will generate you passive income every month while you relax.

The other option that helps you invest in real estate without owning any property is buying shares from a real estate investment trust (REIT). REITs are companies owned by different people, and they specifically use the real estate sector to generate income on behalf of the shareholders. REITs pay higher dividends than other forms of investments.

If you want to generate more revenue from your money, it is vital to choose an appropriate investment that will give you passive income in the long run. However, you should be aware of the challenges you will likely face as a new investor. Other forms of investment come with risks and losses, so you should do your homework first to get more details about the minimum deposit required and compared commissions offered by various brokers.

When you are happy with the services offered by a specific broker, you can open an account. Remember that investing is a long-term process, not a get-rich-quick scheme. If you consistently invest over time, you will reap huge benefits. You need to stick to one strategy no matter what may occur in the market if you want to get more returns from your investment.

Chapter 10: Insurance

Insurance plays different roles in our lives since it's designed to protect us from unforeseen events. This chapter will explain different types of insurance policies and how they help us together with our loved ones. We will also explain how you can choose the best health plan in detail.

What Is Insurance?

An insurance plan refers to a contract between the insurance provider and policyholder in which the latter gets financial protection or compensation for losses from the insurer. A policyholder pays regular premiums to the insurance provider. If you have a policy, your provider will pay you when you encounter an unfortunate incident like an accident, damage to your house, theft, or loss of life.

In other words, insurance plans play a critical role in hedging the policyholder against financial losses that may also result from the actions of third parties. Your plan outlines all the terms and conditions under which the insured party benefits from the insurance provider. You can also use insurance to protect your loved ones.

When you purchase a plan, the insurance provider risks protecting you, and you pay premiums for the services offered. If an insured party experiences any form of eventuality, they can file a claim with their insurance company. An insurance provider evaluates the claim and settles it if the application meets the criteria for approval of compensation.

Benefits of Insurance

In most cases, disaster strikes when you have no money, and this is where an insurance policy comes in handy.

Insurance policies benefit people and society as a whole in various ways. Along with the obvious benefits of insurance, others are not much discussed or discussed. The main advantages of insurance include the following elements.

- **Cover You against Uncertainties** - In the event of unforeseen events like a sudden illness, property damage, or an accident, you will get coverage from your insurer. The protection you get depends on the type of policy you have.

- **Management of Cash Flow** - When you pay for losses caused by uncertainties out of pocket, your finances are likely to be affected. However, when you have the right policy, your insurer will handle the issue, giving you peace of mind.

- **Provides Investment Opportunities** - When you operate a business, make sure you have an appropriate plan. If you want to attract investors, they first check if you have business insurance. If you have no policy, no investor may be willing to risk their money by joining hands with you in business.

Each plan is designed to suit the needs of different people, so you should know what you want.

Types of Insurance

Insurance covers anything, and numerous types of policies are designed to suit different people. No one expects misfortune, but it happens unexpectedly. No single insurance policy can cover everything in your life. Therefore, you will need different types of coverage to prevent financial hardships. Here are the common types of policies you can consider getting protection from different things.

Health Insurance

Health insurance is one of the most critical policies that everyone should have. A sudden medical event can cause serious financial hardships, especially if you pay for your treatment out-of-pocket. The costs are usually so high that other individuals choose to declare bankruptcy when they realize they cannot cover their medical bills.

Medical costs for different treatments are usually very high, and most people without health insurance cannot meet them. However, if you have a health plan, you will get coverage for medical bills, prescription drugs, and physician costs. Your insurer will pay part of the costs, and you should meet your deductible and other out-of-pocket costs. Your policy can make your life easier since it might be difficult to meet your health care needs using your savings.

Life Insurance

A life insurance policy is designed to ensure that your loved ones can live a comfortable life when you are gone. When the breadwinner dies, the designated beneficiaries covered by your life insurance policy will get coverage for loss of financial income. There are different types of life insurance policies, so you should choose something that suits your family's needs. The following are examples of life insurance plans available.

- **Term Life Insurance** - This kind of policy has a specific end date, and you can use it to cover a specific situation.

- **Whole Life Insurance** - This plan provides coverage for your entire life, and premiums will remain the same.

- **Universal Life Insurance** - Offers lifelong coverage, but it is generally cheaper.

- **Variable Life Insurance** - Provides permanent coverage together with cash value. You can choose the sub-account to invest in, and they determine the cash value you will get.

- **Burial and Funeral Insurance** - Mainly covers the final expenses to give the insured person a dignified send-off. If you are in poor health and you don't have another policy, you can consider this plan. You will not leave a burden on your loved ones to look for money to meet your burial and funeral expenses.

- **Survivorship Life Insurance** - The plan ties two people under one plan, and it usually applies to wife and husband. The beneficiaries can get a payout when both holders of the plan are dead. However, you should know the pros and cons of the policy before you get it.

- **Mortgage Life Insurance** - This policy covers the balance on your mortgage when you die. It is designed to protect your family so they will not face challenges in paying the loan. However, the policy does not offer financial flexibility to your loved ones.

- **Credit Life Insurance** - This policy also covers specific debts, and it protects your loved ones if you don't want them to inherit your credits.

- **Supplemental Life Insurance** - Covers a group of people and is inexpensive. However, you cannot own it as an individual, which means you lose it once you lose your job.

Homeowners and Renters Insurance

When you own a property, you must have homeowner's insurance designed to protect your physical structure and valuable possessions against damages that different factors can cause. For example, natural disasters like floods, earthquakes, or thunderstorms can leave a trail of destruction to your property. Other aspects like theft or fire outbreaks can lead to damage and loss of property.

Depending on the type of insurance you have, your insurer can pay for partial damage or cover the repairs for the entire house. Your plan can also cover the damaged possessions in your home. If you are forced to look for alternative accommodation while the house is being repaired, your insurance will cover the expenses.

Renters insurance helps protect the renters' possessions from damage or other aspects like theft. However, you should know that anything can happen at your place, such as unprecedented injuries. If a tenant or a visitor is injured at your property, you will be liable for the damages. To protect yourself from this from lawsuits and medical expenses that may arise from the injury, make sure your homeowner's policy comes with liability insurance.

The main purpose of liability insurance is to cover accidents that may happen at your house. When a guest slips and falls on the stairs in your home, you may be found liable for the injury, and you will be responsible for paying medical expenses. When you have liability coverage, you can mitigate the costs.

Liability insurance also provides coverage to homeowners who may be implicated in accidents outside their homes. For instance, if your dog escapes the yard and it bites someone, your liability insurance will cover the damages.

Disability Insurance

No one wants to be involved in serious accidents that can lead to permanent injuries or disability. However, such incidents are inevitable in some instances. If you work for a corporation dealing with heavy and often dangerous equipment, make sure you get disability insurance. When you suffer an injury that alters your life, disability insurance will replace your salary if you are incapacitated. Most employers provide this kind of policy to their employers to protect them.

It is essential to understand what your disability insurance covers. Other injuries can be life-changing, so disability insurance can go a long way in protecting your interests. Other policies can only pay you during the days you cannot perform your normal work due to the injuries. If the policy is silent about what happens when you suffer a permanent policy, it may give you challenges in the future. Make sure you understand the contents of every policy you get to avoid problems.

Automobile Insurance

If you own a car, you must have auto insurance to protect your car and yourself in the event of an accident. This type of insurance offers coverage for property damage and injuries. When you are involved in an accident, your policy will cover your medical expenses and repairs to your vehicle.

If you are found liable for causing an accident that has led to someone's injuries and property damage, you should meet the medical expenses involved. You can get relief if you have auto insurance that provides third-party coverage. It is illegal to drive without automobile insurance in most states since it helps protect all road users.

Millions of people are involved in an accident every year, and the highest number of insurance claims are for auto accidents in different states. As a general rule, everyone involved in an accident should seek medical attention immediately since other injuries manifest later. Even lighter accidents like stationary collisions will need repairs. If you are at fault, your auto insurance will pay for the repairs of the other party's vehicle. Therefore, the significance of this kind of policy should not be overlooked.

Long Term Care Insurance

If you feel you need to visit nursing homes on either a short-term or long-term basis, you should consider getting a long-term care policy. If you do not have reliable people to look after you, you need this plan. It gives your loved ones peace of mind since you will not expose them to the immense pressure of looking after you.

However, you should know that long-term insurance is expensive since it is concerned about providing specialty services. These come with a high price tag, so you need to consider other alternative options.

Business Insurance

When you operate a business, make sure you get the right policy to protect it against unforeseen events that can lead to financial losses and property damage. Your company can experience natural disasters or other elements like theft which lead to loss of property. There are different types of business insurance available, so you must do your homework to get a plan that suits the needs of your venture.

Accidents and other issues can cause injuries in the workplace. Your business should be protected against all forms of mishaps that can lead to lawsuits or financial loss. Try to establish your needs and look for a policy that gives you enough coverage in your operations.

Other Forms of Insurance

Insurance can cover anything you want, and insurers are ready to provide different services to their clients. Apart from the popular insurance policies highlighted above, other plans are designed to cover specific needs like medical malpractice and professional liability.

With errors and omissions insurance, you can get protection against lawsuits that may arise due to errors in your operations. Medical practitioners are trained to provide quality service to their clients, but mistakes sometimes happen. This is where you need professional insurance.

When you visit different places across the globe, you might need travel insurance. Its main purpose is to protect you against issues like delayed or canceled flights, loss of property, injuries, and other mishaps you may encounter on your trip. Get the right travel policy to enjoy peace of mind when you are thousands of miles away from home.

How to Choose Health Insurance

When choosing an insurance plan, you should understand how it works and suits your needs. There are different types of health policies available, and their differences are marked by mainly three factors explained below.

Premium

When you choose a policy, you should consider its price or premium, paid every month. Your creditworthiness or level of income determines the premium. The insurance provider will check your income to see if you qualify for a particular health policy. The insurance company may also be interested in knowing your credit history to see if you can afford to pay your premiums. Many people use company-provided policies, and these are not complicated. However, if you don't have a work-related health insurance plan, make sure you get something you can afford.

Coverage

Some policies are designed to cover basic healthcare conditions at fair prices. The policy limit also determines the premium. If your policy has a higher limit, you will likely pay higher premiums.

The other aspect that can determine the type of policy you can get relates to any special condition you have. For instance, if you have an underlying chronic condition, it means you will need regular medical checkups. This means your premiums will be slightly higher than other comparable policies. It is essential to check if the policy you want to get covers your condition. It is a good idea to consult your physician to make an informed decision.

Deductible

The deductible refers to the money you should pay out of pocket to get treatment before the insurance company pays your claim. Deductibles help deter people from making unnecessary claims that are usually small and insignificant. If your insurance claim comes with a high premium, you will pay lower deductibles. However, if the policy has high deductibles, it is cheaper. When you make higher out-of-pocket expenses, you will likely make fewer claims.

Insurance plays a critical role in our lives since it protects us from unforeseen eventualities that can cause severe financial consequences. It is vital to protect yourself and your family against financial setbacks that can compromise your future. There are different types of policies available, so you should do your homework and get something that suits your needs. Should know its coverage, deductibles, and premiums when you choose a policy. It is a good idea to purchase the ideal policy for your family and make sure you can afford the monthly premiums.

Chapter 11: Passive Income

In today's world, a single source of income is not sufficient to cover the considerable financial burden. With prices soaring, people are looking for alternative means of earning money. However, people with hard schedules question how to put effort into an additional job. This is where passive income comes in.

People often misunderstand the concept of passive income and how it works and therefore miss out on the many benefits it offers. While active income requires that you put in the time to perform a task or service to get paid, passive income requires little to no effort to generate a consistent cash stream. However, it does require some amount of effort or investment at the beginning of the venture. Almost everyone has some sort of active income in place before deciding to invest in passive income. Like any other investment, passive income sources require some level of commitment, but the generated revenue is all worthwhile.

Reasons for Building a Passive Income Portfolio

Many people don't bother looking into passive income options because they either think it's too much of a hassle or have no motivation to earn passively. However, they are missing out on quite an opportunity, as there are numerous reasons you should consider building a source of passive income.

1. Financial Stability

Many people these days live from paycheck to paycheck and do not have the financial stability to live a carefree life. A source of passive income will help achieve financial stability without spending too much time on a job. This way, you will have a financial safety cushion to lean on and will not have to worry about your paycheck to make ends meet.

2. More Money at Your Disposal

When you're earning passively, there's more money at your disposal to be used to further your finances or just used as you'd like. You can put this extra cash towards savings for your car, your house, or other expenses you'd have difficulty paying with your active income. If money ever held you back from following your passion, getting passive income will solve this problem.

3. Independent of a Paycheck

When you have more financial freedom, you're free to follow your passions without worrying about your paycheck. If you invest in multiple sources of passive income, the more, the merrier.

4. Location Independence

Passive income gives you the freedom to make money from where you'd like. You don't have to be limited to a single location for the rest of your life. In addition to traveling, you can also pick up and move where you've always wanted to when multiple sources of money come in while working remotely.

5. Early Retirement

People living paycheck to paycheck often worry about retirement as little to no options are available for them. However, you can start planning for early retirement with passive income coming in.

Ways to Build Passive Income

Passive income sources either require an upfront time or monetary investment to bring you profit in the long run. If you're not willing to invest in one of these, you can't expect to get a constant money stream at a later stage. This doesn't mean that you have to invest a massive amount of money or months of your time, though; you can start with as little as $5 and put in some effort to get great results. Listed below are some ideas to build a passive income portfolio.

1. Rental Properties

Investing in rental properties is the best way to have a consistent income every month. Rental management companies today make it pretty simple for you to get profits from your rental properties without putting in the time to meet tenets, maintenance staff, etc. While there are a few matters you'd have to give attention to, you also have the option of outsourcing the entire procedure to make this an entirely passive investment.

Depending on your goals and interests, there are several ways you can invest in rental properties to create a source of passive income. Some options include:

- Invest in single-family rentals if you want an easy investment with smooth proceedings. You can even use an online platform to find a suitable property and purchase it.

- If you're looking for a larger scale rental investment, consider investing in a larger development. The best way to do this is to invest in multi-family or commercial properties. You can either fund real estate loans or buy an equity share in a property.

- Farm property is your best bet if you're looking for a less volatile real estate investment. Although it doesn't sound as attractive as the other two options, it's still one of the best options when considering a rental investment.

2. Dividend Stocks

Stock investment is a tried and tested way to earn passive income and generate the most revenue out of all options. It requires time, money, and effort to research stocks, market trends, stock trading tools, and online brokers. The good part is that they generate large dividend amounts. Over time, these stocks generate revenue and provide you with a nice residual income.

Many online brokerages offer stock trading services, various research tools, and other resources. You must do initial research before selecting a brokerage for your stock investing because this is where you'll be investing a lot of your money. With the huge number of brokers present online, the number of scammers is also high, and therefore you should always research and read reviews before you sign up on a platform to invest.

3. High Yield Savings Accounts

If you're looking to generate a safe passive income stream with little to no effort, putting your money in a high yield savings account is your best option. Many banks provide the option of high-interest rates with little to no additional charges. You'll have to do some initial research to find a bank with a suitably high-interest rate and need a substantial sum of money to put in a said bank account.

There's also an alternative to this option where you can put your money in a money market fund. Investment companies manage these, but some banks also provide this option. While bank savings accounts are insured, the same can't be said about these money market funds.

4. Crypto Staking

While you're probably aware of crypto trading and how you can earn profits from it, there are chances you haven't heard about crypto staking. Crypto trading is an active income generation technique, whereas crypto staking doesn't require much work and is considered a passive source of income. And, like other investments, this option is associated with some risk.

Crypto staking involves delegating your cryptocurrency to someone verifying activity on an underlying blockchain network by compiling records of transactions. These verifiers need to put some crypto tokens at stake to protect against fraud transmissions. If they're successful, you get some share of their rewards. But, there's also a risk involved when you put your tokens at stake. Plus, you can't sell or trade your tokens for some duration.

5. Annuities

Annuities can be good options for having a consistent passive income stream but have some complicated conditions. In essence, they are considered to be an insurance product that you pay for, and in turn, you'll be paid a consistent amount every month for the rest of your life. Doesn't that sound please? But before you get too excited, know that these investments are not suitable for every individual as they require a high initial capital investment. On the other hand, this option is great if you have a zero-risk tolerance policy, ensuring zero loss. Therefore, you must consult a financial advisor before you invest in annuities.

6. Real Estate Investment Trust

If you're interested in real estate investments but don't want to deal with the hassle of buying and managing properties yourself, investing in a real estate investment trust (REIT) is the right thing to do. This way, you'll also be able to avoid having to pay the hefty down payment and any maintenance or fixing charges that may pop up. A real estate investment trust is pretty similar to mutual funds where they purchase and own commercial property, including offices, retail buildings, hotels, and apartments. REITs pay a high dividend amount, but before you decide to invest in REITs, research the technicalities associated with investing in these ventures.

7. Peer-to-Peer Lending

P2P lending involves you lending your money to people who do not get approved for traditional loans. While this option has a considerable amount of risk involved, the interest rates associated with P2P lending can be somewhat attractive. The good thing about this option is that there are various platforms dedicated to this exact purpose where you can simply sign up and start investing money without having to worry about payback. These platforms ensure you get paid back with additional interest amounts in ample time. As the lender, you will have the freedom to choose who you lend your money to and the payback time.

8. Create Content

Content creation is one of the biggest passive income sources in today's world. Most global businesses are looking for opportunities to create content and get it to their audience. Once you get your audience's attention, you can start cashing out your content by directly selling it, monetizing it, and displaying advertising. This will get you payments for the use of intellectual property that you own the rights to. However, creating content can take up a significant amount of time, but once this time and effort are invested, there's a steady stream of revenue generation for a long while. the attention of your audience. Content creation ideas can include:

- Start a blog.
- Create a YouTube channel.
- Develop an app.
- Design a website.
- License music.
- Create a course online.
- Sell stock photos.
- Write an e-book.

9. Affiliate or Network Marketing

Affiliate and network marketing is becoming increasingly common as a side hustle for many people. It helps them get a decent amount of money while not putting in constant effort. However, like many other investments, this option requires you to initially put in effort and keep a watch on it. Affiliate marketing gets you commissions every time a user reaches your sponsor's product page through your content. However, building content and a loyal customer base can take a lot of time.

On the other hand, network marketing can provide a better option for earning passive income by creating a downline team. With each of their sales, you get a percentage of their commission.

10.   Storage Rentals

Storage rentals can get you a decent amount for little to no effort at all. You need to purchase or rent a property, specifically a warehouse-type property, and put an ad for your storage rental. Now, all you have to do is wait for your customers to reach you and ensure they've stored their things inside the rental. This will get you quite an amount, as people often need storage space for the furniture and other things they've accumulated.

11. Pay Off Debt

If you manage to pay off or even reduce your debt, you will be saving an appreciable amount of your income. And, like other things, this too requires an initial investment. The good thing about paying off debt is that it gives you a good return on investment. For instance, if your credit interest is 10%, paying off your debt would mean you'll get 10% straight back. There are two ways you can go about paying off your debt; these include:

- Refinancing or consolidating your debt. For instance, refinancing is better if you're under student loans, whereas credit card debt should be consolidated with a personal loan.

- You can also try bank transfers or simply pay down your debts.

12. CD Ladders

Building CD ladders is a complicated but low-risk investment for a passive revenue opportunity. You can get a higher return on investment if you buy certificates of deposits (CDs) in certain increments from the bank. This is a great option for people who want to avoid risky investments at all costs.

13. Dropshipping

Dropshipping is one of the simplest passive income sources on this list. It's also the most profitable and easy to understand. If you're unfamiliar with the world of dropshipping, it's simply an international business on popular platforms like AliExpress. You can start a dropshipping store, find trending products, and sell them to your international audiences. The best part about dropshipping is that it gives you the flexibility to price your products and control many other aspects of your business. You can use a wholesale marketplace to obtain your products and then sell them to your customers. Although this gets you a reasonable income, it also requires quite a lot of time and effort. So, if you're willing to spend some time on your dropshipping business, you have a promising revenue generation opportunity.

14. Use Passive Income Apps

What's more passive than going through your daily routine while getting paid for it? Well, that's exactly what passive income apps are designed for. These apps are usually used for market research and data collection. They track your day-to-day activities and sell this data to interested parties. Don't worry; it doesn't violate your privacy or any private information. All you need to do is install these apps on your phone, register for their rewards, and forget that it exists until you need to get paid. Some apps may give you easy tasks like walking a certain distance every day or exercising.

There's nothing better than having the financial freedom to pursue your passions or spending time pursuing your hobbies. However, with the economic strain on most people, this becomes nothing more than a dream. This is why it's important to have more than one source of income, and that too a passive income. Passive earning gives you all the benefits of a job, but without having to put in a lot of work. However, nothing comes without a price, and getting passive income sources requires some initial investment, whether of your time or money. But, once you've established a suitable solution for this, you'll have peace of mind regarding financial constraints. There are many more techniques for earning passive income in addition to the ones listed above. With each technique, there's some capital or time investment required. No one said earning money would be easy, but it can be a little less challenging with passive earning.

Conclusion

Very few people are ready to make financial decisions, especially as they grow more and more complex over time. Financial illiteracy should not be as common as it is, and it's the main reason many people are crushed under financial burdens these days. How to properly save and invest should be common knowledge, yet only several people pay attention to the details concerning these subjects.

The rapidly changing technology hasn't made it easier for people to get a hold of managing their finances either. But with passing time, this technology will only evolve further, and thus the need for financial literacy will increase considerably. The importance of financial literacy, therefore, cannot be understated.

To plan and manage your finances efficiently, an individual needs a thorough understanding of relevant concepts, evaluate where their financial mindset is, and then move towards topics like budgeting, saving, and investing. It's important to track your spending to understand where the majority of your finances are going. This is also when you'd need to identify wasteful spending and look for ways to eliminate it.

Next, you need to establish a personal financial plan, which is somewhat like a professional financial plan. It considers your income, spending, savings, any investments you might have, and other important financial information. Identifying these parameters will help you set a budget, as explained in the book, and you will need to stick to this budget to manage your cash flow efficiently.

The use of technology is also very important if you are to manage finances effectively. The internet has many resources and financial tools available, both free and paid. These tools will make it considerably easier for you to develop a financial plan, calculate expenses and taxes, and even help save money.

Many people are buried under debts. Be it student loan debt, credit card debt, or simple loan debts. High-interest rates don't make it easier to pay back loans on time. Understanding how loans work, which loans would be suitable for you, and how you can pay them off quickly is key to staying out of debt.

In addition to understanding which bank and bank account would be the most suitable for you, you should also be aware of the difference between the various credit and debit cards available. It's essential to learn this difference; otherwise, you may make many bad financial decisions. Investing should also be an essential part of your financial plan. It brings you a stream of passive income, but it also broadens your financial sources. Even when investing, you must have a diverse portfolio consisting of several different investments. Putting all your money in the same place has never worked out for anyone.

In the end, there are many considerations you will need to make when planning your budget and managing finances. Just ensure you do all that with an open mind and keep working on opportunities to improve your financial well-being.

References

guest. (2021, June 2). Why personal finance is crucial in everyday life. The Financial Express. https://www.financialexpress.com/money/why-personal-finance-is-crucial-in-everyday-life/2263454/

Hayes, A. (2022, February 8). Fiscal Policy. Investopedia. https://www.investopedia.com/terms/f/fiscalpolicy.asp

Kurt, D. (2022, April 4). What Is Finance? Investopedia. https://www.investopedia.com/ask/answers/what-is-finance/

Sharma, K. A. (2014, May 8). 5 simple stories every financial professional can use. Don Connelly & Associates. https://donconnelly.com/simple-stories-financial-professionals/

Why financial literacy is so important. (2015, October 6). Investopedia. https://www.investopedia.com/articles/investing/100615/why-financial-literacy-and-education-so-important.asp#toc-why-is-financial-literacy-important

Why financial literacy is so important. (2015, October 6). Investopedia. https://www.investopedia.com/articles/investing/100615/why-financial-literacy-and-education-so-important.asp#toc-why-is-financial-literacy-important

Cruze, R. (2021, December 22). How to set financial goals. Ramsey Solutions. https://www.ramseysolutions.com/personal-growth/setting-financial-goals

Muller, C. (2018, July 23). 5 simple steps to evaluate your financial health. Money Under 30. https://www.moneyunder30.com/simple-steps-to-evaluating-your-financial-health

Pajer, N. (2021, October 20). Is your relationship with money holding you back? Shondaland.

https://www.shondaland.com/live/money/a38006576/is-your-relationship-with-money-holding-you-back/

10 Reasons you need a financial plan. (n.d.). Canarahsbclife.Com. https://www.canarahsbclife.com/blog/saving-plan/10-reasons-you-need-a-financial-plan.html

Agrawal, N. (2018, August 16). Why financial planning is important for your future? Entrepreneur India. https://www.entrepreneur.com/article/318528

Example of A financial plan to help you create yours. (2021, July 9). Clever Girl Finance. https://www.clevergirlfinance.com/blog/example-of-a-financial-plan/

Mint. (2020, October 26). How to create a financial plan in 11 steps. MintLife Blog. https://mint.intuit.com/blog/planning/how-to-make-a-financial-plan/

More, R. (2018, May 14). What is a financial plan, and how can I make one? NerdWallet. https://www.nerdwallet.com/article/investing/what-is-a-financial-plan

N. (n.d.). Personal financial planning—tips on setting yourself up for the future. N26. from https://n26.com/en-eu/blog/personal-financial-planning

Qayum, A. (2020, November 19). How to create a personal financial plan (and reach your goals faster). Oberlo.Com. https://www.oberlo.com/blog/financial-plan

Synovus. (2018, May 16). 6 reasons why you need a financial plan. Synovus.Com; Synovus Financial Corp. https://www.synovus.com/personal/resource-center/investing/6-reasons-why-you-need-a-financial-plan/

Zhu, E. (2020, August 27). What is a financial plan, and how do you build one? SmartAsset. https://smartasset.com/financial-advisor/what-is-a-financial-plan

Bell, A. (2022, April 7). 6 reasons why you need a budget. Investopedia. https://www.investopedia.com/financial-edge/1109/6-reasons-why-you-need-a-budget.aspx

Bieber, C. (2018, April 21). Budgeting 101: How to start budgeting for the first time. The Motley Fool. https://www.fool.com/investing/2018/04/21/budgeting-101-how-to-start-budgeting-for-the-first.aspx

Caldwell, M. (n.d.-a). 8 reasons you need an emergency fund. The Balance. https://www.thebalance.com/reasons-you-need-an-emergency-fund-2385536

Caldwell, M. (n.d.-b). Understanding budgeting & personal finance. The Balance. https://www.thebalance.com/personal-finance-budget-4802696

Dunn, E., & Norton, M. (2014). Happy money: The new science of smarter spending. Oneworld Publications.

Four Reasons Emergency Funds are Important. (n.d.). 1Stunitedcu.Org. https://www.1stunitedcu.org/more-for-you/financial-wellness/four-reasons-emergency-funds-are-important

Habits, B. M. (2022, March 29). How to create a budget in 6 simple steps. Better Money Habits; Bank of America. https://bettermoneyhabits.bankofamerica.com/en/saving-budgeting/creating-a-budget

Jain, M. (2021, March 2). How to save money from salary? The Money Club. https://moneyclubber.com/blog/how-to-save-money-from-salary/

More, R. (2017, November 30). Emergency Fund: What it Is and Why it Matters. NerdWallet. https://www.nerdwallet.com/article/banking/savings/emergency-fund-why-it-matters

Vohwinkle, J. (n.d.). Your 6-step guide to making a personal budget. The Balance https://www.thebalance.com/how-to-make-a-budget-1289587

What is Budgeting, and Why is it Important? (n.d.). My Money Coach https://www.mymoneycoach.ca/budgeting/what-is-a-budget-planning-forecasting

Latham, K. (2022, March 28). Can tech help you to manage the cost of living? BBC News. https://www.bbc.com/news/business-60680531

Dore, K. (n.d.). Best budgeting apps. Investopedia https://www.investopedia.com/best-budgeting-apps-5085405

SDFLC. (2015, October 9). 4 ways technology has impacted the personal finance world. San Diego Financial Literacy Center. https://www.sdflc.org/2625-2/

Chen, J. (2022, April 5). Debt. Investopedia. https://www.investopedia.com/terms/d/debt.asp

How to pay off debt faster. (n.d.). Wellsfargo.Com. https://www.wellsfargo.com/goals-credit/smarter-credit/manage-your-debt/pay-off-debt-faster/

How to pay off debts fast - 25 practical tips from finance experts. (2022, March 21). GoodtoKnow. https://www.goodto.com/money/how-to-pay-off-debt-656900

Landon, D. (n.d.). How to pay off debt: 3 strategies and 6 tips. Bankrate. https://www.bankrate.com/personal-finance/debt/how-to-pay-off-debt/

More, R. (2019, May 28). 6 things to know about student loans before you start school. NerdWallet. https://www.nerdwallet.com/article/loans/student-loans/6-things-to-know-about-student-loans-before-freshman-year

When should you consider filing for bankruptcy? (n.d.). LendingTree. https://www.lendingtree.com/bankruptcy/when-should-you-consider-filing-for-bankruptcy/

Bennett, K. (n.d.). The best credit unions of 2022. Bankrate https://www.bankrate.com/banking/best-credit-unions/

Bennett, R. (n.d.-a). How to choose A bank: 8 steps to take. Bankrate. https://www.bankrate.com/banking/how-to-choose-a-bank/

Bennett, R. (n.d.-b). Understanding the different types of bank accounts. Bankrate. https://www.bankrate.com/banking/types-of-bank-accounts/

Brandon Renfro, C. F. P. (n.d.). What is an overdraft fee, and how do you avoid them? Bankrate. https://www.bankrate.com/banking/checking/what-is-an-overdraft-fee/

Frankenfield, J. (2022, March 24). Online Banking. Investopedia. https://www.investopedia.com/terms/o/onlinebanking.asp

Kopp, C. M. (2022, February 8). How interest rates work on savings accounts. Investopedia. https://www.investopedia.com/articles/personal-finance/062315/how-interest-rates-work-savings-accounts.asp

More, R. (2018, February 13). Is online banking safe? How to boost your banking security. NerdWallet. https://www.nerdwallet.com/article/banking/online-banking-security

Taylor, K. (2022, April 28). How to choose a bank. Investopedia. https://www.investopedia.com/how-to-choose-a-bank-5183999

The advantages of personal internet banking. (2021, July 20). First United Bank & Trust. https://mybank.com/the-advantages-of-personal-internet-banking/

BankBazaar. (2017, August 1). Difference between Credit cards and debit cards. BankBazaar. https://www.bankbazaar.com/credit-card/difference-between-debit-and-credit-card.html

Nesvig, K. (2021, October 19). 7 common myths about credit cards (and what financial experts want you to know instead!). Apartment Therapy; Apartment Therapy, LLC. https://www.apartmenttherapy.com/common-credit-card-myths-36989170

White, A. (2020, January 6). What is a good credit score, and how to get one? CNBC. https://www.cnbc.com/select/what-is-a-good-credit-score/

More, R. (2018, May 23). What is a good credit score? How do I get a good credit score? NerdWallet. https://www.nerdwallet.com/article/finance/what-is-a-good-credit-score

What is the time value of money, and why is it important? (n.d.). Attune Financial Planning. https://attunefp.com/blog/what-is-the-time-value-of-money-and-why-is-it-important

Irby, L. (n.d.). The dangers of credit card debt and how to avoid them. The Balance. https://www.thebalance.com/dangers-of-credit-cards-960217

First State Community Bank. (n.d.). Improve your finances with 7 money management tips. Fscb.Com. https://www.fscb.com/blog/7-money-management-tips-to-improve-your-finances

More, R. (2019, July 25). How to invest in stocks. NerdWallet. https://www.nerdwallet.com/article/investing/how-to-invest-in-stocks

Smith, R. (2016). Investing for beginners: A beginner's guide on how to make money by investing in stocks and mutual funds. Createspace Independent Publishing Platform.

Kagan, J. (2022, February 8). Insurance. Investopedia. https://www.investopedia.com/terms/i/insurance.asp

What is insurance? (n.d.). Maxlifeinsurance.Com. https://www.maxlifeinsurance.com/blog/term-insurance/what-is-insurance

Wrights, C. M. (n.d.). What is insurance? The Balancefrom https://www.thebalance.com/what-is-insurance-5209926

Luzzatto, J. (2020, June 23). The seven types of insurance every person needs. Forbes. https://www.forbes.com/sites/forbesfinancecouncil/2020/06/2 3/the-seven-types-of-insurance-every-person-needs/?sh=6be3117898fe

Farrington, R. (2022, January 1). 35 passive income ideas you can use to build real wealth. The College Investor. https://thecollegeinvestor.com/16399/20-passive-income-ideas/

Ferreira, N. M. (2020, November 19). 23 passive income ideas to build wealth in 2022. Oberlo.Com. https://www.oberlo.com/blog/passive-income

Meyers, S. (2021, July 6). 6 amazing benefits of earning a passive income. Passive Storage Investing. https://passivestorageinvesting.com/6-amazing-benefits-of-earning-a-passive-income/

More, R. (2020, April 14). Passive income: 10 ways to make money while you sleep. NerdWallet. https://www.nerdwallet.com/article/investing/what-is-passive-income-and-how-do-i-earn-it

Murphy, R. J. (2018). Passive income: 2 Manuscripts - affiliate marketing for beginners, dropshipping for beginners. Createspace Independent Publishing Platform

www.ingramcontent.com/pod-product-compliance
Lightning Source LLC
Chambersburg PA
CBHW071655210326
41597CB00017B/2215